MEANINGFUL LIVING

MEANINGFUL LIVING

Logotherapeutic Guide to Health

Elisabeth Lukas
Translated from the German by Joseph B. Fabry
Foreword by Viktor E. Frankl

An Institute of Logotherapy Press Book

Grove Press, Inc./New York

First Evergreen Edition 1986
First Printing 1986
ISBN: 0-394-62166-2
Library of Congress Catalog Card Number: 86-228

Library of Congress Cataloging-in-Publication Data
Lukas, Elisabeth S.
  Meaningful living.
  Translation of: Auch dein Leben hat Sinn.
  Reprint. Originally published: Cambridge, Mass. :
  1. Logotherapy. I. Title. Schenkman, ©1984.
[RC489 1986]   616.89'14   86-228
ISBN 0-394-62166-2 (Evergreen : pbk.)

Printed in the United States of America

GROVE PRESS, INC., 196 West Houston Street
New York, N.Y. 10014

5 4 3 2 1

Acknowledgment

I wish to express my sincere thanks to the anonymous donor in San Francisco who made the publication of this book possible.

Elisabeth Lukas

Acknowledgments

Contents

Foreword ix

1. Our Search for Meaning 1

2. Causes and Consequences of Existential Frustration 19

3. Premises and Methods 27

    Modification of Attitudes 33

    Paradoxical Intention 36

    Dereflection 39

    The Appealing Technique 40

4. The Application of Modification of Attitudes 43

5. The Application of Paradoxical Intention 73

6. The Application of Dereflection 89

7. The Application of the Appealing Technique 113

8. The "Ideal" Logotherapist 129

Foreword

"What? Another book on psychology? Don't we have enough?" Admitted: Psychology has become suspect. It has been fractured into sects, it is an industry. The sects are becoming ideologies and commercial enterprises.

However, readers will notice how this book by Elisabeth Lukas differs from the literature flooding today's market, how it radiates compassion! The ingenuity with which Dr. Lukas discovers—and inspires—humaneness in the most desolate cases! Her case histories rehumanize psychotherapy in its best sense.

This book is not only human, it is also honest. Contrary to many of her colleagues who claim to know it all, the author admits the limits and weaknesses of her work, thereby gaining credibility. She gets rid of stereotypes and counteracts the cynicism so prevalent in psychology today. Some passages should be shouted from the rooftops!

For Lukas there is no human being who does not retain a chance to grow, no situation which does not have its spark of meaning. How dramatically this is done is witnessed in moving testimonies.

To elucidate meaning possibilities is the art of Elisabeth Lukas and entirely in the tradition of logotherapy. Meaning is at the center. People are helped in their search for meaning, the most human of all human concerns—fighting the meaninglessness that has become something like a mass neurosis.

The more acute this feeling of meaninglessness, the more timely logotherapy is. In the sixties Gordon Allport of Harvard University called logotherapy "the most significant psychological movement of our day." A decade later the *American Journal of Psychiatry* referred to logotherapy by asking, "What could be more pertinent as we enter 1970?" Now in the eighties the same question is discussed in *The International Forum for Logotherapy*. (Cf. Arthur G. Wirth, "Logotherapy in the Post-Petroleum Society," Spring 1980).

In this book Elisabeth Lukas draws from her rich and long experience as a practicing logotherapist and head of a psychological counseling center in Munich. There, at the dawn of the "post-petroleum" society, she works with patients struggling with the typical problems and crises of our age. Her testimony is scientifically grounded. At every step we sense her empirical training.

She began with experimental research and statistical investigations. To her we owe the first logotherapeutic test in the German language, the logotest, developed at the Institute of Experimental Psychology of the University of Vienna. Here practical experience and empirical research are combined in productive feedback reactions.

Her contributions are not limited to basic research. She creates imaginative logotherapeutic techniques like the "naive questions technique" or the expansion of the logotherapeutic method of dereflection. In case histories we accompany her to the future of logotherapy.

Most constructive perhaps are her glimpses into the logotherapeutic workplace. Every point is illustrated with case histories including verbatim dialogues. Repeatedly she provides readers with the tools to apply logotherapy to their own lives, and it is amazing what successes become possible. I possess ample evidence that people who suffered for years from severe neuroses and were treated without success were cured by applying logotherapeutic methods learned exclusively from books.

Edith Weisskopf-Joelson, professor of psychology at the University of Georgia, shows that logotherapy can be applied as self-help. She states that, contrary to other books in this field, books on logotherapy are directed less to psychotherapists than to patients and other readers who are not (yet) neurotic: They can apply the ideas of logotherapy to themselves, sometimes making the intervention of a professional therapist unnecessary. As she states, books on logotherapy are "bibliotherapy." ("The Place of Logotherapy in the World Today," *The International Forum for Logotherapy*, Spring 1980).

Some years ago I heard a lecture by Elisabeth Lukas and was deeply impressed. I told her: "Somehow it is easier to know I'll die—being assured that my legacy rests in your hands." A few years later I read the manuscript of this book and felt deeply reassured. I read the manuscript in a hospital bed and, for a time, even in an intensive-care unit. When I finished I felt proud of a student who made me hope that I have not lived in vain.

Boston, on my 75th birthday   Viktor E. Frankl

MEANINGFUL LIVING

1

Our Search for Meaning

The search for meaning is as old as humanity. It is perhaps the prime characteristic distinguishing human beings from the rest of the animal kingdom. Although the search has been with us from the beginning, it is critical in our twentieth century because now, particularly in the West, we have liberated ourselves from many shackles. We have gained unprecedented areas of free space for ourselves, but have not achieved the maturity to handle it.

Our problem with meaning is indeed linked with the question of freedom. For many, freedom has positive connotations. We long for it but forget that we can lose our way in unstructured freedom. We are free to walk in any direction; there are no barriers. But neither are there guideposts to a goal. In an open field we can get lost easily.

Here are some of the shackles from which we have liberated ourselves.

For centuries parents chose marriage partners for their grown children, or at least influenced that choice. Marriage took place for social or economic reasons, often disregarding the children's wishes. Today, the West has gone through a revolutionary change—free choice of partners according to our needs and wants. Yet this is when the institution of marriage has become questionable. According to statistics, every second marriage seems to be a mistake. More freedom of choice has brought greater insecurity.

Another example is the place of woman in the West. She has broken the traditional shackles of being "just a housewife and mother" and has won the freedom to practice almost any profession. But this freedom has its price: She faces the double or triple pressure of taking care of the home, rearing the children, and establishing herself in a profession. Thus in finding personal fulfillment severe conflicts arise between family and professional responsibilities.

Other examples (such as the use of leisure time) are not the immediate result of our crumbling traditions. Modern technology has increased our free time and comfort. We do not always know what to do with our free time, and comfort tempts us to an increasingly passive life. We sit in front of our TV set and a remote-control button spares us the effort of getting up to switch channels. The illusion of everlasting comfort relaxes but tends against productive activities. We even have a new profession, that of "leisure counselor." Our spiritual horizon is shrinking, liberation from work has made many people *prisoners* of modern comfort.

Hardly any liberation has been more dramatic than that from sexual restrictions; and in no area is insecurity greater. An abundance of sexual stimuli has promoted the belief that sexual potency and orgasms are musts—and opened the floodgates of sexual dysfunction. Natural needs are artificially emphasized at the cost of human caring and affection. The result has been dissatisfaction, an inability to love, and disgust.

Equally dramatic are the consequences of liberation in the upbringing of children. Never before have children had so much freedom and power over their parents. They are raised without guidance, without role models, and with almost no restraints; and never before have we experienced such demoralization, aggressiveness, or reaction of young people against themselves and their environment. What lies behind this brutality? What is to be done with all that free energy? What goals are still worth pursuing? Our children's self-understanding is undermined: the entire family suffers from the loss of "social control" which before was exerted by a large circle of relatives and friends. People live isolated in huge apartment houses. They are free to do what they want, but life has lost its attraction: a metropolitan desert threatens sanity.

Contemporary art, liberated from traditional rules, is in a chaos of sudden freedom. The formless has become the form of our century, the unesthetic and the incomprehensible are the expression of artistic revolution. Freedom from all rules has become *the* rule in the arts.

A final example: the gradual disintegration of religious allegiance. Theories and philosophies, hypotheses and speculations are born and die as fast as fashion changes. The result is disenchantment and a clinging to what seems secure—the rational, the materialistic. But the downgrading of myths and ideals is only the façade. Behind it is a permanent state of insecurity and skepticism that seems incurable.

If freedom results in insecurity, does this mean we should have no freedom? No; it means that we need the maturity to make meaningful use of it. As with all values, freedom has practical applications which must be understood. Suppose a movie pregnant with meaning is shown on television. In front of the screen sits a two-year old, bored. To the child the movie is a sequence of disconnected color pictures. It cannot perceive the totality because meaning lies in the interrelationships between apparently disconnected parts. Similarly, human freedom has value only to the extent that our maturity allows us to see the total picture.

Human beings are in constant development. The question then is: If freedom requires a certain maturity, how can we achieve it and speed up our growth process?

Growth cannot occur in shackles—neither in the rearing of children nor in the evolution of a whole species. Even if the beginning is chaotic, only by experiencing freedom can we acquire the maturity to handle it. This is no time for pessimism, pessimism prevents us from seeing the specific chance offered by our confused twentieth century—the chance to reach a higher level of maturity.

As I tell my despairing patients, every crisis has its opportunity. This is also true of crises arising from our striving for freedom. Perhaps *this* crisis will speed up maturation. Understanding freedom as responsibility would be a giant step indeed.

Our general crisis is revealed in the suffering of disturbed patients, in the strange mixture of aggressive, depressive, and self-centered people who in spite of having plenty to live *with* have lost the assurance of what to live *for*.

Viktor Frankl realized years ago that psychiatry today confronts problems different from those his teachers and predecessors dealt with. He perceived a worldwide feeling of meaninglessness gripping an increasing number of people. The more luxury and freedom, the more anxiety. People ask themselves what they should do with their affluence and whether this could really be the ultimate meaning of life.

Industrial society, bent on ever-increasing production, puts enormous pressure on people to consume in order "to be happy."

Happiness is owning a dreamhouse with two bathrooms and a big car, whether needed or not. Happiness is a daily orgasm stimulated by films, magazines, and expensive sex treatments. Happiness is offered adolescents and even children through alcohol and hallucinogens. The latest wave of "happiness" comes in the form of brutality, senseless crimes, and political power plays. We talk much about the pursuit of happiness—how little is found in people's hearts today!

What weighs on them is doubt about what awaits them at the end of this long and feverish chase for happiness, what meaning lies behind all that stress and striving for prestige and material gain. The time-tested answers, including those of religion, are buried under crumbling traditions. Beliefs are no longer trusted, intuition is darkened, and the prevalent philosophies offer only doubt. Only when we understand these developments, in society as well as individuals, can we respond to the cries for help in our patients.

PEOPLE IN DOUBT

In today's psychotherapeutic practice we face two large groups of people in need of help, neither necessarily sick. One consists primarily of young people but includes older ones who have retained some adolescent insecurity. I call these "people in doubt." To them everything seems negative and questionable. They are searching for a goal to pursue, an idea to believe in, a task to fulfill because they find themselves in a horrendous emptiness which Frankl has termed the "existential vacuum." They see no purpose in their lives and are searching for meaning. There is nothing sick about this search; on the contrary, probably every person has to go through this stage to find a personal value system to reorient goals and life content.

If this search for meaning gets stuck in a permanent state of doubt and no further growth takes place, serious neurotic, psychotic, or depressive consequences may result.

Case #1:

A father came to our counseling center with his 22-year-old son. As soon as they were seated they began to shout at each other before I had a chance to find out what the problem was. I arranged separate interviews.

The father had founded a well-established firm and planned for his son to take over. The son graduated in business administration and gained practical experience by working in another firm. Now about to enter his father's firm, the son suddenly lost interest in a business career. He withdrew to his room, brooded, and refused to join his father's enterprise. In his anger the father talked about disowning him.

The son said nothing except that I wouldn't understand him anyway. Only after great effort was I able to get an explanation. He didn't see any point in taking over the father's business. He was interested in neither its continuation nor in its profits. Why slave away his life to sell things people could buy elsewhere? What was the sense of it all? What was the sense of anything he had done so far? Everything was fruitless and contemptible. His impulse was to run away and never come back.

The young man was full of doubts about himself and the world, searching for meaning, while his father had his life goal in his firm. But what holds meaning for one person is not necessarily true for another, and what is readily attainable too easily loses its value.

I advised them both, as a start, to break the cycle of hostility in which they were caught. Maybe a prolonged trip abroad would help the son clarify his feelings. This trip was to be undertaken not for pleasure but with the firm intent to search his conscience and find possible goals for his life. Would he find it attractive to work in his father's firm in some other capacity—for instance, in the creation of a research department or the supervision of personnel? If not, what other job would seem meaningful and yet realistic? We came to a compromise between father and son: The father was willing to finance the trip and, in exchange, would expect his son to come home with plans for his future. The father promised to respect his son's plans whatever they might be, while the son promised to devote all his efforts to attain his goal. To counteract the son's present doubt in the meaning of life, we placed the focus on his search.

It was not easy for the father to agree to this compromise, and yet this was the best chance for both. For the father, it offered the chance to love and respect his son even if the latter should decide not to work in the firm; for the son, it offered the chance to break the cycle of doubt and find his personal life task.

PEOPLE IN DESPAIR

The second group of people, whom I call "people in despair," are not necessarily sick either. They once had a meaningful life orientation but either lost it through a blow of fate or now find it insufficient or disappointing. This group includes people who have lived a lifetime of pleasure, power, or wealth, and realize they pursued a *non sequitur* and now feel empty. This realization might provide the impetus for new directions and attitudes for which it is never too late, or it might lead—as psychotherapists well know—to resignation, a feeling of meaninglessness, and even to thoughts of suicide.

Stanislav Kratochvil, psychologist at the municipal clinic in Kromeriz, Czechoslovakia, presented at the 1968 World Congress for Mental Health in London a theory about value and meaning orientation. Building on Frankl's logotherapeutic principles, he divided people who have found a value orientation into two groups: those who have found security in a "parallel" and those who have found it in a "pyramidal" value system.

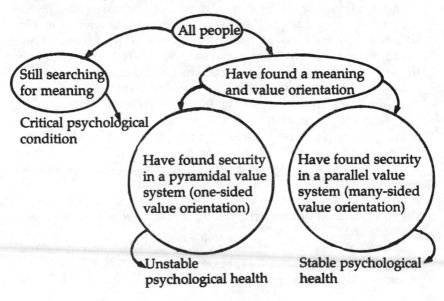

Kratochvil describes people who are secure in a parallel value system as having several equally strong values in their lives, all meaningful; for instance, a man who has found fulfillment in his work and his family, and is also enjoying his hobbies and finding fulfillment in his religious faith. These are parallel values contributing to his meaning orientation.

In contrast, in the pyramidal value system, one large value is at the top while the others rank far below, so the total value system is arranged like a pyramid. Those secure in this system see only one goal worth striving for, one interest worth pursuing; for example, a man who finds fulfillment in his profession neglecting everything else, or a mother who lives only for her children and shuts out the rest of the world, or a servant of God absorbed in prayer, disregarding worldly tasks. There are also those who give themselves to accumulating wealth, making a career, or carrying out political or philosophical tasks.

People in either group are happy and have a sense of meaning; they do not suffer from inner emptiness. Still, Kratochvil proved that people with a parallel value orientation were healthier and more stable than those with a pyramidal one. He states two reasons for his conclusion:

1. If the chief value in a pyramidal value system topples, the whole life concept is in shambles. A mother who has lived exclusively for her children has no other values to fall back on when the children grow up and leave home. The workaholic forced to retire may become sick, bored, or irritated because there is nothing meaningful left. The religious person who loses his beliefs is lost. If the top value is shaken or breaks off, lower values are not significant enough to take its place.

In a parallel value system it is much easier to replace the loss of one value by others of equal significance. The man who must retire but has a satisfactory hobby is happy to have more time for it and will not experience sudden emptiness. The woman who besides her obligations as a mother has her own social life will see her children's independence as an opportunity to do more things with her friends. A parallel oriented value system provides options and allows for compensations to shape life anew.

2. People who hold only one value high or "true" tend toward fanaticism and intolerance. The mother who lives only for her chil-

dren finds it difficult to understand another who places her child in a childcare center so she can pursue a career. The workaholic does not easily understand someone not primarily interested in a career and "wasting" his time on hobbies. The religious fanatic is tempted to convert others and condemns "unbelievers." People with a pyramidal value structure do not get along easily with others who have divergent values, and may treat them aggressively or contemptuously.

People with a wider value spread find it easier to form interpersonal relationships. The man who loves his wife and children, finds fulfillment in his work, has a hobby that fascinates him, enjoys mountain climbing and playing music, has a greater understanding for a diversity of people—for the concerned parent, as well as for the amateur gardener, the nature friend, or the enthusiastic musician.

In sum: Frankl distinguishes two groups of people: those still searching for meaning ("people in doubt") and others who have found meaning through their personal value system. Kratochvil subdivides the latter into those who have found meaning through a parallel value system, and those who have found it through a pyramidal one. Those with a pyramidal value system can lose their footing when their principal meaning is threatened ("people in despair").

To Case #1:

Suppose in a family constellation as in Case #1 the father's primary value lies in his self-established business. It is the top value of his pyramid. If the son refuses to take over the firm, the business cannot stay in the family; it will have to be sold. The top of the pyramid becomes more precarious the older the father grows. He must ask himself whether his life's work has not been meaningless—a short step to despair.

The psychotherapist cannot force the son to take over his father's firm. But she can assist the father to widen his value system and to raise some of his lower values so they can take over the meaning orientation if the top value—the firm—topples.

This means the psychotherapist must help the patient trans-

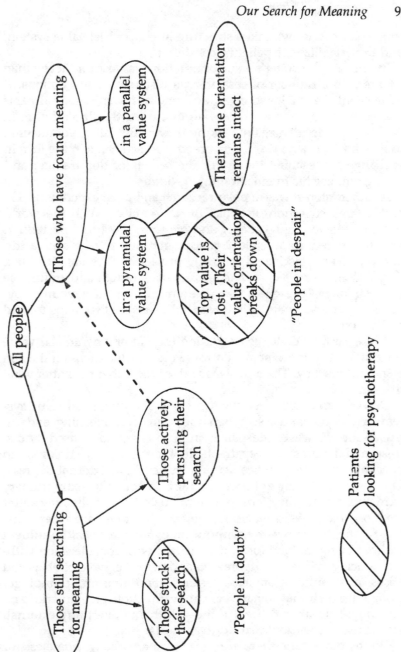

All people

Those who have found meaning

in a parallel value system

in a pyramidal value system

Their value orientation remains intact

Top value is lost. Their value orientation breaks down

"People in despair"

Those still searching for meaning

Those actively pursuing their search

Those stuck in their search

"People in doubt"

Patients looking for psychotherapy

form the existing pyramidal structure into a parallel value system, and thus stabilize the patient's condition.

In our case the father's value orientation was less top-heavy than I feared. In a number of sessions we discussed other options. It turned out that he loved dogs, and one of his childhood dreams was to be a dog trainer. When we discussed the firm's future in case the son decided against taking it over, the father volunteered to give a friend who was a dog breeder some shares in the firm in exchange for teaching the father the secrets of dog training and letting him use his friend's training grounds.

Another interest was in polar research and polar expeditions. He had a large collection of books on the subject. With the world becoming increasingly smaller and his sound financial position, a visit to a pole was possible. I encouraged him to take such a trip and he became fascinated with the project. "I'll be able to ride a dog sled and have a chance to admire the strength and endurance of polar dogs," he cried with the enthusiasm of a young boy. These, of course, were only ideas; but ideas are first steps toward realizations.

These Socratic dialogues—shifting the father's pyramidal value orientation to a more parallel one—were concluded when the son began his journey. The basis was laid for the father no matter what the son would decide.

Despair can occur when the top value of a pyramidal value system breaks off, and also when the search for meaning ends in frustration. However, despair is in most cases not caused by distress and failures. Few patients in mental health clinics or in psychotherapeutic practice actually suffer from external distress. They are not starving or homeless; they do not suffer extraordinary hardship, nor are their jobs too strenuous. Occasionally they suffer from organic or psychological problems, but these are exceptions. Most patients are healthy without enjoying their health, affluent without being grateful for it, and treated with consideration without noticing it. They are depressed and neurotic, have phobias and obsessions, suffer from sleeplessness and tension, cannot get along with their mates, have sexual dysfunctions, feel inferior and dependent, weak and tired of life—all this without any external, visible reason, without real troubles or distress.

On the other hand there are those who are needy, homeless, or on welfare; laborers with large families and hungry children living in crowded quarters who are psychologically healthy. They "have no time" to be neurotic or suicidal, and no money for expensive therapies.

Some say poor people don't seek therapeutic help because they can't afford it. My experience has shown otherwise. For years I have worked in public counseling centers that offer therapy at no cost to anyone who has problems with children, marriage, jobs, or with him or herself. But our caseload is by no means confined to the poor. Those seeking help (and this is also true for other free clinics) are mostly middle or upper class, outwardly doing fine. They could be happy but are not. The reason is that they are increasingly in doubt about their meaning in life or they have lost it. Albert Einstein once said that "A person who thinks his life has no meaning not only is unhappy but is hardly fit to live."

SUCCESS AND MEANING

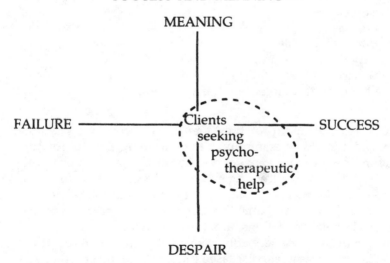

As Frankl indicated many years ago, success does not equal meaning, nor failure despair. Meaning is found by many people who have not achieved success, and those in pain and sickness can still say "yes" to life despite everything. But there are also those who are tortured by doubt and inner emptiness at the height of outer success.

The illustration on page 11 is based on statistics of 500 clients in nonlogotherapeutic counseling centers. Every client was placed in one of four quadrants, depending on their "success"—career and personal relationships, health, lucky breaks, etc.—and sense of meaning. The largest number, some 80 percent, turned out to be in the lower right quadrant, consisting of people in despair (or doubt) despite outward success.

Years ago I made up a test that measured the degree of meaning a person experiences. The test was developed after 1,000 people in various sections of Vienna were asked which value meant most to them. We established these nine categories:

Personal well-being (happiness)
Self-actualization
Family, children
Career
Friendships
Interests, hobbies
Experiences (nature)
Service in a cause
Overcoming distress (hunger, sickness)

This list (testimony of the "man and woman on the street") confirmed Frankl's assumption that meaning can be found not only in activities and experiences, but also through one's positive attitude toward a distressing situation. To transcend unavoidable tragedy is a human achievement of high meaning potential.

I learned from my patients what a human being is capable of even in hopeless situations, and never have I felt more admiration than for those who were able to overcome their severe suffering. Here are two examples, discussed more fully later: a mother whose only and very much wanted child was born mentally retarded worked on herself for years to accept this fact and finally found a positive attitude toward her situation (Case #4); a young woman whose face was grotesquely misshapen after a car accident and whose husband left her, rediscovered her courage to live (Case #20).

Distress does not inevitably cause psychological collapse; it may contain the possibility of finding new meanings. The psychotherapist today sees that to solve conflicts it is not always essential to dig up childhood traumas or to focus on our unhappy past. It may be more important to widen and strengthen the inner meaning orientation of clients so they can grow from distress situations instead of being defeated by them, to discover potentials and become more mature. Hence a true alternative is offered by humanistic psychotherapies such as logotherapy. Instead of exploring the past for reasons clients say "no" to life, they are helped to find paths where they can say "yes" to life in spite of all that happened. If distress situations contain possibilities of meaning, then lack of distress situations eliminate some possibilities. This may be the reason neuroses and depressions are more frequent in affluent societies than where people have to struggle for their survival.

Of course, psychotherapists need not reduce affluence to reduce neuroses. What they can do is make their clients aware of additional meaning possibilities by widening their horizons. Therapists cannot give meanings; they can only guide their clients through the darkness of doubt and emptiness, and illuminate the guideposts. It is up to the clients to choose the path.

Case # 2:

A 24-year-old woman came to see me because "her nerves were completely shot." She had married young because she was pregnant. Her husband had come from a prominent family. She herself had been brought up in modest circumstances by a single parent and felt inferior to her husband and his family. They made her feel that she had pushed herself into the family only because she was pregnant. The marriage ended in divorce and custody of the son was given to the father because his family could provide for him better. The young woman was confronted with having to evaluate her past and decide her future. She felt unable to cope with what was left in her life and sank into despair. She longed to see her son but did not dare use her visitation rights because she was afraid to meet her ex-husband's family.

Here was a starting point for my therapy because for the sake of a child a mother is able to draw on unsuspected strength, and that's what was needed: strength, especially strength of the spirit.

Nothing helps more to gain inner health than the strength to defy fate, to apply one's "defiant power of the human spirit."

I told the young woman that I understood how unpleasant it was for her to meet with the parents of her ex-husband, but that she had the obligation to visit her son because he would wonder about his mother and suffer from her sudden disappearance. Then I made a suggestion to her. How would it be if she would meet her relatives in a new role when she picked up her son? Not as the timid and dejected person they knew, but as a self-assured young woman who didn't allow herself to be defeated. This would not only gain the respect of the family, but would make her feel better about herself, and actually make the visit pleasant. She would have to play this "role" only once a week, and do it for the sake of her child. After some hesitation, the woman agreed and we "rehearsed the performance."

At our next session she looked quite satisfied. Everything had gone well and she had gotten a kick out of seeing the surprise of her ex-in-laws. "We can surprise other people, too," I told her. "Your friends will expect you to knuckle under because of what happened to you, and will be amazed if you don't." "But I can't continue playing this role, I don't really feel this way," she protested. I explained that she was a person with all sorts of unrealized capabilities, and that her confidence had been deeply buried after her many experiences of failure. The "acting as if" technique, I told her, would not work if she would pretend to be something she was not, but that in her case it worked because it made conscious, even for a little while, a part of herself that had been repressed.

The "acting as if" method was but a part of the therapy plan. We then started to consider various possibilities for her to find new paths to meaning, new goals. "We will now think about various possibilities and ways to spend your life until you find one which seems right for you," I told her. I asked her to sit back and close her eyes and listen while I outlined a number of possibilities which might suit a woman of her age. When I described a day in the life of a woman who helped in a kindergarten doing arts and crafts with the children and preparing snacks for them, she perked up: "Yes, I think that would be a good thing to do. I'd love to do something like that."

We now had to find a good way to reach her goal, or at least approach it, such as helping in a baby clinic or babysitting. It was amazing to see her change. She lost much of her hopelessness and eagerly planned the steps toward her new goal.

"You know, I may even have the chance to see my child more often," she said. "I could take him along to kindergarten while I work there." Focusing on her future pulled her out of her despair. She applied for jobs and was accepted as a helper at a day-care center. Before the interview her courage left her but we succeeded by "rehearsing" the role of a self-confident applicant. Once she got the job we extended her search for meaningful goals by exploring what she could do in the evening, after work. She could not see herself living in her tiny apartment without a partner. She said, "the ceiling falls on my head."

Again we looked at her options. Blushing, she confessed that she had thought of placing a lonely-heart ad in the newspaper. We considered the pros and cons, and concluded that she would save the money to go to a reputable matrimonial agency. While she was trying to save money, she met a young man. Half a year later she sent me a wedding announcement and added a few lines: "Dear Dr. Lukas, I am doing fine and may even go back to school to become a professional kindergarten teacher. Hans (my husband) loves children and gives me a lot of support. My son is growing up nicely and my ex-in-laws are now quite friendly. I think they realize that I was not as unfit as they thought. Maybe everything that happened was for the best, otherwise I would have remained a housewife and never met Hans. Thanks for helping me through my worst time . . ."

MATURITY AND MEANING

This is a simple example to show how a widening of meaning choices can overcome despair. Unfortunately, in practice it is not always easy to use this approach because the psychotherapist has to contend with a powerful enemy: immaturity.

We all go through a lifetime of learning and development, a process that slows down in later years. Along with this learning and growing is a maturing characterized less by an increase of knowledge than by experience and understanding.

In former times the advice of older people was appreciated, and not without reason. Old people have learned from life; they may be forgetful and retell their experiences many times; they may not understand much that is new, but often they have a maturity and balance when young people are still groping.

In my practice I often found a close correlation between meaning orientation and maturity level. Building on Kratochvil's distinction (p. 6) I would say that the search for meaning corresponds to the early stage of human development, the pyramidal value orientation to the mid-stage, and the parallel value orientation to the later, mature stage of life. Thus the main reason for today's desperate search for meaning is not so much a sudden meaninglessness, as a delayed maturing of our generation, especially compared with our rapidly growing intellectual and technical skills. It also means that every person goes through all three phases: a general search for meaning, the discovery of a single important meaning, and eventually the realization that many meaningful tasks are waiting. Psychological instability and neurosis result when maturing is arrested or when we revert to a previous level.

Years of working with children and adolescents have convinced me that maturation to a diversified and positive value system is quickened and less painful when parents provide a broad and many-layered educational foundation at an early stage. This makes the search for meaning easier for children who follow the model of their parents. The meaning of work, for instance, can be demonstrated by parents as a value and task rather than as a means to make money. Children need to know what their parents are doing at work and what it means to them. Equally important is the meaning of leisure activities—doing things together, enjoying art and nature, being creative in gardening, tinkering, painting, or playing. Children who see their parents watching television, reading the sports page, or going to a bar, may as grown-ups copy them because they see no alternative. If children see parents do volunteer work, charitable deeds, work in politics and other causes that seem important, these can become guideposts to a meaningful life later.

Many young people today are spared the challenges that contribute to early maturing. It's not their fault that they grow up in an era of affluence. They have no appreciation for the abundance that has fallen into their laps. No amount of scolding will make them healthy. We must offer them new meaning choices.

But to offer does not mean letting them do as they please, and meaning choices are not unlimited freedom.

A healthy upbringing requires that the freedom allowed corresponds to the maturity level. I often see the difficulties that arise when "freedom" is given to children too early. Parents let small children do what they want, fulfill their every whim, and are permissive and indulgent. These children, when in their teens, become egotistical, lazy, bored, and unwilling to do their homework. *Then* the fathers suddenly become strict, ground them, limit their TV time, and cut their allowances. Mothers, too, scold and nag, rules are given, and freedom is restricted. This reversal is harmful in the educational process and not likely to lead to good results.

The adolescent child does not know what to do with freedom. It needs guidelines and simple rules in order to find orientation. It needs role models, value patterns, stimulation, leadership, example, because the basic structure of the adult's meaning options is laid during this early stage. As children grow through and beyond puberty they increasingly need more freedom to develop their personality and assume more responsibility.

Here we come back to our initial concept of freedom. True human freedom is never freedom "from" but always freedom "to" something. Freedom goes beyond release from rules and guidelines by outer authority. Its corollary is the freedom to follow inner authority—self-chosen tasks, commitments, goals. Freedom is not doing as we please but pleasure in doing what we consider meaningful. If freedom is exercised arbitrarily, without responsibility, the result is not meaning but chaos. Only with maturity is freedom meaningful—the freedom to make responsible decisions about what we think, do, and refuse to do. Then life is no longer an open field without roads and signposts where we wander aimlessly. Mature people carry their signposts within and are able to find their own orientation. They need the open space to reach the many goals they have chosen. Maturity is a decisive precondition.

In the West we are discovering something despite—or perhaps because of—the gap between too much freedom and not enough maturity. We find that pleasure and affluence alone do not bring happiness, that inner satisfaction comes with finding meaning in our own conduct. This is an enormous step in development even in the midst of a search-for-meaning crisis.

I want to end this chapter with a note of hope for the twentieth century. The great inner confusion and dissatisfaction of our generation, this desperate search for meaning we experience today, may speed up the maturing process so that some day we shall be able to base our lives on meanings and values rather than on arbitrariness, power, egoism, and material gain. Humanity's crisis today may be its opportunity for tomorrow.

2

Causes and Consequences
of Existential Frustration

During the last thirty years scientists, physicians, and psychologists have encountered a new type of neurosis that cannot be attributed to such traditional causes as repressed sex drives, a frustrated hunger for power, or faulty learning processes. Such explanations no longer make sense in our liberated and affluent societies where the young have more sexual freedom and power than ever before and enjoy, by and large, better educational opportunities than any previous generation. Yet they are not happy.

Viktor Frankl was the first to diagnose and describe this new syndrome, and in 1950 named it "existential frustration." It manifests itself in boredom, indifference, feelings of meaninglessness, inner emptiness, a lack of goal orientation, apathy, despondence, and dissatisfaction with life. It affects young people sitting in discothèques sipping beer, immersed in loud music from the juke box and staring for hours in the air. It affects dope users who, all keyed up, spend all night in confused discussion. It affects men and women who indiscriminately have sex with each other, just for the thrill of it.

Grown-ups too, are afflicted with existential frustration. They change careers, try this and that, without finding satisfaction. They chase after money and material things, and when they have accumulated property, do not know what to do with it. They escape from reality into dreams, into alcohol, kill their Sundays in front of television, or seek in abnormal sex practices a gratification that escapes them. They are satiated with everything, and satisfied with nothing, and in the end they say: "I am sick of living."

Existential frustration, the feeling of meaninglessness, is usually accompanied by a feeling of inner emptiness which Frankl terms "existential vacuum." Social research has shown that this vacuum may have dangerous consequences. Among them are depression,

19

"inflation of sex," addiction, and violence. Also the frightening attraction of cults may be a result of the existential vacuum.

Logotherapy recognizes these connections and shows why traditional methods of psychotherapy are ineffective. To cure and prevent worldwide meaninglessness is not a matter of psychotherapeutic method or of a mere interpretation of symptoms. It is a matter of defining a new concept of human nature. Frankl shows that the concept of human nature in traditional psychology misses the most important dimension, the "specifically human dimension" of the spirit. As all other animals we are, of course, dependent on conditions and needs, on drives, environment, and learning processes. At the same time we live on a higher level where we see and understand our dependencies and conditions, and can take a stand toward and even against them. It is in the human dimension—containing cognition, attitudes, and the "will to meaning"—that the motivational laws of psychoanalysis and behavior therapy are found insufficient.

In our human dimension we are not primarily concerned with satisfying drives, finding inner equilibrium, reducing stress, and gratifying pleasures, as older theories assumed. Here we are motivated by our "will to meaning" (as Frankl calls it)—a reaching out for activities and experiences meaningful to us. If we are determined to reach a self-chosen goal, devote ourselves to a task, make a cause our own, or lovingly reach out to another person, we are prepared for sacrifices, to disregard drives and forego pleasures. And we are happy because we have an inner satisfaction and see meaning behind what we do or give up: we see a reason for our sacrifices.

On the other hand, if we can satisfy all our drives, nothing is demanded of us; if we live in affluence without seeing a meaning in life, we become existentially frustrated, psychologically ill, or severely neurotic and depressed. To understand such phenomena we have to revise our concept of human nature.

The logotherapeutic concept of human nature takes our longing for meaning into account. The logotherapist does not disregard our physical and psychological conditions, our drives, the importance of childhood, environment, and upbringing. But these influences are supplemented by the assumption of a dimension in which we can take on a task for its own sake, not just to release inner tension, gratify a need, or respond to social pressure. Logotherapy replaces the nihilistic concept that we are "nothing but" an evolved animal, a product of chance, with the positive idea that we are "essentially more than."

I will clarify the logotherapeutic concept of human nature through a parable:

Imagine sitting in a concert hall listening to a piano sonata by Beethoven. To produce this wonderful piece of music a piano is necessary, because without an instrument even the most exquisite composition cannot be heard. The physical presence of the piano is needed but is not enough. In this sense it can be compared to our body. What the sonata also needs is a pianist with the ability to play the composition without mistakes. But even piano-plus-pianist is not enough to perform the Beethoven sonata. The pianist can perform, but without the score the meaningful flow of sounds is missing. Arbitrarily played sounds do not produce a harmonious musical structure. The ability of the pianist to play the keys is comparable to our psychological functions which influence the body but have no higher and meaningful content. Now the dimension of the spirit comes into the picture: the composition. Only the composition unites the piano and the pianist into a meaningful totality; it makes the piano important as the carrier of the music, and it enables the pianist to transform an idea into a beautiful acoustic experience. In the same way spirit brings about a meaningful interplay between body and psyche. When the composition has been played to the end and the last sound fades in the concert hall, piano and pianist become single factors again; the union is dissolved.

This parable illustrates the danger of reducing human nature to a mere physio-psychological dimension. It is as if we had said: Music is "nothing but" hitting keys, or music is "nothing but" steel strings.

Logotherapy rejects this reductionism and asserts that the human being is far more than just an electro-chemical substance driven by psychologically determined behavior patterns. It points to the additional dimension of the spirit which unites body and psyche in a meaningful entity, just as the composition coordinates the singing strings of the instruments and the skilled fingers of the pianist.

This medically new concept of the human being led to a new interpretation of symptoms: The worldwide existential frustration can now be seen as a consequence of an "underdemanding" of the human spirit causing psychological symptoms even when the person lives in affluence. Logotherapy has confirmed the observation by Schopenhauer that people fluctuate between two extremes: distress and boredom. Distress is ᴄaused by worry, malnutrition, early aging, poor medical care—that is, by physical danger. Boredom, on the other hand, is caused by existential frustration and a feeling of meaninglessness—that is, by psychological danger.

Case #3:

A well-situated man turned to me for help with his 48-year-old wife. She had never touched a drop of alcohol but had recently taken to the bottle, especially when he was not home. And this was often the case because as an executive of a wine company he had to take frequent business trips.

My talk with the wife revealed that the couple had a 27-year-old son who was working in the firm's central office in France and only seldom came to Germany. The father met him occasionally on his business trips but the mother saw him only once or twice a year.

During the past three years the couple had built a beautiful home in a wooded area. The woman had been busy overseeing the work, being in charge of the inside decoration and the selection of furnishings. She had created a rustic hunting room widely admired by their friends. Now the home was complete and too large for two people, especially since the husband was away often. She wandered through the large and carefully furnished rooms all by herself with nothing to do. She was gripped by sudden attacks of anxiety, by a feeling of emptiness and uselessness which only a glass of wine could temporarily fill.

As long as she had to take care of her son and as long as her home needed her attention she could see meaning in her existence, and she remained psychologically healthy. But with the son gone and the home completed she saw no purpose in her existence and no substitute in sight because the most expensive property is no substitute for the satisfaction of a meaningful life.

I decided to tell the husband the truth as I saw it, and suggested the following: As long as his wife sat in the "golden cage" of her home there was the danger of depression and alcoholism. How would it be if she would accompany him on his business trips and be given small responsibilities such as making hotel reservations, arranging evening events with his business partners, perhaps letting her be in charge of customer lists, or similar assignments? He might tell her that, getting on in age, he could use a helper on his travels. The man objected; these trips would be too strenuous for his wife who was not in the best of health anyway. But I expressed my conviction that her preoccupation with her health was the result of an existential frustration and that it would fade away when she widened her meaning horizon. Hesitating, the man promised to try my suggestion.

I didn't hear from them for a long time. Then, one day, the man came to my office with a bouquet of flowers. His wife was well and cheerful. She enjoyed the trips and also enjoyed coming home which they now appreciated fully. "And what about the drinking?" I asked. He had to think for a moment, then laughed: "Oh, that! That's no problem. A little glass of wine now and then, that's all."

CONSEQUENCES OF EXISTENTIAL FRUSTRATION

I have listed, as the main consequences of existential frustration: depression, indiscriminate sex, addiction, and crime. That a feeling of meaninglessness and inner emptiness may lead to depression is easy to see. If we see no meaning, consider ourselves as "nothing but" a little collection of organic matter that vegetates until it dies, if we draw our balance sheet in a way that shows us more sad and indifferent hours than happy ones, we are bound to come to the conclusion that life is not worth living. A life just to stay alive makes no sense. Only human beings are able to realize that and, therefore, suffer from it.

The other three consequences of existential frustration can also be explained by Frankl's concept of human nature. Indiscriminate sex is an attempt to fill our inner emptiness with physical pleasure. Drugs give us the illusion of meaning, and crime provides us with goals, albeit destructive ones.

Sexual excesses have often been associated with affluence. My history teacher pointed out that the refinement of clothing had always been a measuring stick for the affluence and decay of a society. The flimsier and more transparent the materials (even in antiquity), the richer and closer to downfall was the nation. Was this hypothesis valid today? Transparent clothes mean greater attention to sexuality, a more intense pursuit of pleasure, and—paradoxically—a more widespread sexual dysfunction. The more people are intent on sexual pleasure, the less they are capable of attaining it—a paradox well-known in clinics and counseling centers, confirmed today by the high incidence of impotence and frigidity. Can the "incapacity to love" be attributed to the existential vacuum? Possibly. If we truly love our partner we are not likely to plunge into existential frustration because our love provides at least one path to meaning.

Addiction, another form of the pursuit of pleasure, also misses its aim. The intoxication solves the problem of meaninglessness because the distorted world of the addict seems to open new dimensions but the return to reality is all the more disappointing. The addicts pass by their true tasks and goals while they live in a delusive world of a temporary, harmful, and possibly deadly intoxication.

According to current statistics, today's crimes have undergone a change. Rarely do thieves steal because of hunger and burglars rob because of real want. Luxury merchandise is shoplifted, windows are smashed, property is vandalized, and people are killed for a few dollars. Many crimes are committed merely for the thrill to fill an empty life.

Then there are terrorists who desperately try to reach a goal by whatever means possible, even if it means killing the innocent. These are people with a pyramidal value orientation. But even in a pyramidal value system, the goal and sense of responsibility must be in accord in order to achieve meaning. If the gap is too wide it opens the way to fanaticism. Fanatics, as Frankl defines them, are people who do not have an opinion; the opinion has *them.*

These are some of the consequences of existential frustration on a social level. On a personal level we find these symptoms in every psychotherapeutic practice. Worldwide research has shown that 20 percent of all cases of psychological illness are caused not by childhood traumas and past conflicts but by an existential frustration and value conflict. (In logotherapy we speak of "noogenic" neuroses). In the remaining 80 percent, depression, sexual neurosis, addiction, and psychopathology play a part which has potential links with existential frustration. This is why we need a therapy that responds to the distress factors of our time. Frankl's work has not only revised the concept of human nature and found a new interpretation of prevalent symptoms (in society as well as in individuals) but has developed effective methods to treat existential frustration and its consequences.

This book deals with these methods in a practical way. It probes these methods from all sides: the empirical, practical, therapeutic, and philosophical, to see how they can serve therapists, as well as lay people who wish to apply logotherapy in their own lives. I shall show the possibilities of logotherapy and admit its limitations. My courage may bring me opponents. I hope my honesty will appease them.

3

Premises and Methods

The practical application of logotherapy is based on one axiom and six premises:

Axiom: The human being has a specifically human dimension—the spirit. It is also called the "noetic" dimension, from the Greek word "noos" (mind), an exclusively human characteristic.

Premise 1: The human being is three-dimensional (assuming that the first two, body and psyche, are granted).

Premise 2: In each of the three dimensions dependency on given circumstances is different: Within the biological dimension (shared with animals and plants) dependency on given circumstances is almost total and hardly manipulable. Within the psychological dimension (shared with animals) dependency on given circumstances is flexible and highly manipulable. Within the dimension of the spirit (exclusively human) there exists the possibility of a free choice of attitude toward given circumstances.

Premise 3: The three dimensions form an inseparable unit.

Premise 4: No dimension can be disregarded in psychotherapy. Psychotherapists must treat their patients in their totality, including all dimensions. Surgeons must not confine themselves to the amputation of a leg when a patient suffers from bone cancer. Nor must psychologists restrict themselves to an interpretation of test results when their clients question the meaning of life. Ministers must not limit themselves to religious wisdom when members of their congregation come to them with family problems. All members of the helping professions have an obligation to respond to genuine calls for help, if not on a professional then on a human level. If they feel incompetent in a certain area, they should refer patients to others who can provide help.

Premise 5: The feedback mechanism works differently in each of the three dimensions. Within the biological dimension, feedback mechanisms bring about automatic processes in the automatic nervous system that help the body adapt to a changed situation. Within the psychological dimension, feedback mechanisms bring about reinforcement processes and lead to changes in behavior. Within the dimension of the spirit, feedback mechanisms bring about changes in self-understanding and lead to a new interpretation of the self.

Premise 6: For each of the three dimensions the principle of homeostasis has a different validity. Within the biological dimension the homeostasis principle is always valid. Within the psychological dimension, it is valid most of the time. Within the dimension of the spirit, it is not valid.

Nearly all theories about human nature see homeostasis, the absence of tension, as a desirable therapeutic goal. Frankl, however, points out that in the dimension of the spirit homeostasis is not a desirable condition but rather a warning signal of existential frustration. A tensionless state in the spirit would denote complete satisfaction, a lack of goals. Goals beckon only when conditions are *not* completely satisfying and leave room for change. When people lack the necessity to change, to create, to finish a project, to experience, or at least to brave unchanging fate, the need to live may be questioned.

Frankl speaks of a "healthy noodynamism," a field of tension between what we are and our vision of becoming. Such noetic tension stands in opposition to being in balance with ourselves and the world. Balance is enormously important for all life forms, but for human beings it is not enough.

Case #4

A 34-year-old mother of a mentally retarded boy sought my help so her child could lead a life as close to normal as possible. He was eight years old, hardly able to stand up, crawled on the floor on all fours emitting inarticulate sounds. He spent the day in a kindergarten for retarded children but the mother feared that nothing was done there to help him develop. She worried about what would happen to the child after she and her husband died. The case history and my observation of the boy convinced me that, considering the severe cerebral damage, nothing more could be done for the child. Deep inside, the mother knew this yet went from doctor to doctor to find out what still could be done, and everywhere she was told that further efforts would be in vain. I, too, could have sent her away because I was not "competent" for cases of brain damage.

But I sensed that the real distress of the mother was on a different level: She could not accept the cruel and unjust fate of having given birth to a mentally handicapped child. As I cautiously explored the question, the entire load of the suffering mother came to the surface. She did not want to admit to herself what became increasingly obvious: that there was no hope to rehabilitate her child to something near normalcy. The woman had to learn to accept her fate as unavoidable and find some positive aspects in it. Only then would she stop running from institution to institution and seeking help from experts who were "not competent." Then, together with her retarded child, she would find inner peace and perhaps even happiness. And so our talks took, for her, an unexpected turn, aimed not at a possible improvement of the child but at a new attitude in the mother. It became a search for meaning, a struggle for a different interpretation of fate that would enable her to accept that fate even if it was cruel. We had to find an answer to that infernal question: Why?

Our talks lasted a long time but one day came to a turning point. "You know," she told me, "I really am no longer afraid of the future. Other mothers have to let go of their children when they grow up, but I can keep my child as long as I live. And after that, someone will take care of him. My husband and I have prepared ourselves for a long life shared with our son—we will not be alone. And we'll always know what we are here for, won't we?" Her eyes were moist but there was a smile on her lips, and I knew I could conclude the counseling. She had begun to accept the retardation of her child and to find a positive approach to it.

THE FEEDBACK EFFECT:
SOME NOTES TO PREMISE 5

Attention to the feedback effect links logotherapy to behavior therapy. Behavior therapy works mostly on the psychological level using positive and negative reinforcement. For instance, when the therapist nods approvingly every time a mother says something good about her child, the mother is prompted to praise the child more often and her positive statements are reinforced. Behavior therapy uses the feedback mechanism to produce changes in behavior.

Logotherapy uses the feedback mechanism in the human dimension to bring about changes in self-understanding. What we learn from outside sources we accept intellectually; but it also influences our self-interpretation. For instance, a doctor's statement that a patient's condition is serious not only serves as information, but may also induce a feeling of hopelessness which can undermine the patient's health. Then the doctor's statement is no longer true because the patient's condition, through the new self-interpretation, is no longer serious. It has become hopeless.

Another example: A survey is published disclosing that every fourth student has tried drugs. The impact of this information on the self-understanding of many students will be: "If so many others try drugs it can't be all that bad, and I can try them too." And one day the statistic is no longer true: Not every fourth, but every third student is experimenting with drugs.

This "feedback paradox" has the effect that a true fact told to us may lead to a changed self-understanding and become untrue. Similarly, a false fact told to us may, through a changed self-understanding, become true.

Simple examples of the feedback paradox are the effects of placebo and suggestion.

Case #5

A mother brought her eight-year-old boy because every morning he felt nauseous in the school bus even though no organic causes could be found. Some talks with the child revealed that he was afraid of a boy who sat next to him in the bus and who teased and intimidated him. The boys were separated and he sat next to a friend. Nevertheless, his sickness persisted; he was already "conditioned."

I tried the following method: I gave the boy a box with innocent tablets and told him they were sure-fire pills against his bus nausea. He was to take one pill a day for a week, then a pill every two days for another week, and a pill every three days for a third week. After that he would be cured. I very seriously admonished him to take the pills conscientiously, or they would not help. In addition, I asked him to watch passing cars from the bus and write down those with consecutive numbers on their license plates. Every day he was to bring me his "best find," the longest string of consecutive numbers. This distractive maneuver (an application of dereflection which will be discussed later), together with the suggestion of a cure, brought about a change in his self-understanding. Although this suggestion was based on a false statement, it made the nausea disappear. The false information had become true as a result of the feedback mechanism. The innocent pills had really "cured" the boy. His conviction that he no longer could become sick was stronger than his psychosomatic difficulties.

Of course, the effects of the feedback mechanism cannot be used in medicine indiscriminately. A cancer victim cannot be cured by placebo pills. The therapeutic feedback process does not exist on the biological level. On the psychological level it *is* possible, and it is aimed at a change of behavior. On the level of the spirit, it is aimed, as stated before, at changing self-interpretation.

An example of the striking effect of the feedback mechanism on the level of the spirit is the well-known experiment by Jacobson and Rosenthal. After testing hundreds of school children for their IQ they did not tell the teachers the true results but gave them a list of the "most intelligent" children who had been determined by lot. Three years later a new test showed that the children who had arbitrarily been labeled "intelligent" actually had a higher IQ. This experiment made many psychologists uneasy because they asked themselves if they had not condemned many children (and adults too) to lifelong "stupidity" by releasing the true results of the IQ tests to the teachers.

The results of the Jacobson-Rosenthal experiment have been widely interpreted as a transferred feedback effect. The false information had been given not to the children but to the teachers. Apparently this made the teachers expect more of the "intelligent" children; perhaps they worked with them more intensively, gave them more difficult tasks, praised their achievements, and in general demanded more of them. This had a feedback effect on the children so that they responded to the expectations and demands with a greater effort, all unconsciously and unintentionally.

These and similar experiments have shaken my original conviction that a psychologist must tell the patients the truth and nothing but the truth. I have learned that psychologists carry a heavy responsibility in what they say and how they say it, and that it is often better to formulate the truth cautiously rather than to be frank about it and bring about a deterioration of the situation.

This responsibility also applies to the way psychologists present human nature since it will influence their patients' self-understanding. If human beings are pictured as dominated by their childhood experiences, many persons with unhappy childhoods will be led to believe that they have been permanently damaged, and this belief will *really* damage them. If symptoms are given a mechanistic interpretation, the patients' attention is turned toward mechanistic processes. An analytic interpretation directs their attention to the gratification of needs and drives. A logotherapeutic interpretation of human nature educates patients to recognize tasks, values, and responsibilities.

Logotherapy does not claim dogmatically that life has meaning, and our motivation is predominantly meaning oriented. Logotherapy has discovered, however, that people who see meaning in their lives and are able to find goals, tasks, and values, are psychologically healthy and stable, while others who find their lives empty tend to become sick and despairing. *This* is the reason logotherapy stresses a view of human nature which includes a dimension of the spirit with its will to meaning, goal orientation, and awareness of responsibility so that this concept of the human being—whether true or not—creates a positive feedback in our self-understanding and thus, through a new self-interpretation, becomes true.

Logotherapy is open to interpretation. Its effectiveness does not depend on special techniques that must be applied under all circumstances. It provides basic concepts that pervade every therapy plan. The rest is techniques, improvisation, intuition, and the right word at the right moment.

Among the logotherapeutic techniques four are prominent:

Modification of attitudes
Paradoxical intention
Dereflection
The appealing technique

These four methods are briefly outlined here. Their practical applications are presented later.

MODIFICATION OF ATTITUDES

The importance of our attitudes toward ourselves, our lives, and our difficulties has been a crucial discovery of psychotherapy. The personal attitude toward their lives and their problems is especially decisive for clients in that gray area between psychological sickness and health who fill our clinics and counseling centers. Indeed it is often their unhealthy attitude, and not the problem itself, that causes their distress.

No one is without problems. We all carry our burdens, but they do not make all of us sick. On the contrary, problems and burdens can activate our human forces; they offer the conditions under which we can show what we are capable of. An unhealthy attitude can block inner forces which could overcome suffering and distress, and push us into a passive role in which we feel that we are the helpless victims of our difficulties.

We also experience a "sunny side" of life—good fortune, a life without worries lived in affluence. These conditions are prone to activate our positive aspects. If we are healthy and well off we can accomplish more than if we are sick and struggling to make a living. And we are also in a position to help others.

But here, too, an unhealthy attitude can block our positive forces and push us into the passive role of the hedonistic pleasure seeker, a role which does not bring fulfillment as is shown by worldwide existential frustration.

An unhealthy attitude is always in some ways linked with passivity, negation, resignation, and often with despair, stagnation, and indifference. I am more concerned when my clients show a profound indifference than when they are in deep despair, because I know that a way out can be found for suicidal persons in despair.

But when they want to throw away their lives out of indifference, they are lost.

Case #6

An example of an unhealthy attitude would be a mother who says: "With this boy I have nothing but problems. He is from my first marriage, his father was no good, and the boy is going to be like him." This negative attitude toward her former husband is enough to turn the boy into a problem child. The unfortunate attitude of the mother freezes the boy in a hopeless situation. In the eyes of his mother he is unable to develop in a positive direction. A vicious cycle is set in motion: the unhealthy attitude of the mother has the feedback effect of developing real behavioral problems in the boy, which in turn confirm the mother's belief that the boy is a troublemaker.

Case #7

Another example of an unhealthy attitude would be a young man who, after having been fired from two jobs, calls out in despair: "I am no good. All my brothers and sisters are successful, but I am a failure." His resignation blocks all efforts of will; but only a great exercise of will and stamina could free him from his dilemma.

Case #8

A wife complains: "It's hopeless to talk to my husband. He doesn't understand me." This attitude blocks all possibilities of an approach; it prevents all chances for a new beginning of a communication between the two.

The therapeutic goal is to redirect the clients' attitudes toward new thoughts and insights that will help them find positive, psychohygienically healthy attitudes.

To Case #6

Sometimes arguments are sufficient to set in motion a modification of attitudes. The mother who blames the problems of her child on her ex-husband may be told that behavior is influenced by parents, but not in the way she imagines. Characteristics, talents, and tendencies may be inherited from parents but not as good or bad qualities. The natural endowments of a child are steered by upbringing and environment into socially desirable or undesirable behavior, and this is primarily in the mother's hands. The counselor must make it clear to her that any undesirable behavior in the boy is not predetermined by his father, but that she herself has a great influence on the direction her child will take and that it is her responsibility to lead him in the best possible direction.

To Case #7

Sometimes arguments are not enough. They must be backed by the positive philosophy of the counselor and, when necessary, by positive suggestions. To the young man who was ready to give up after two failures, the counselor may say emphatically: "Every person has gifts in some areas, and not in others. We'll find out (for instance, through a psychological test) in what direction your talents lie, where you will find your place. When we know that, we'll put all our energy to work to find a job in that field—and you'll see, then you *cannot* fail." This approach will rekindle his courage and confidence.

To Case #8

Sometimes a simple "trick" helps modify attitudes. The wife who claimed her husband did not understand her, was told to make a list of her husband's positive qualities. At the next counseling session she brought a piece of paper on which she had written: "He doesn't play around, doesn't drink, plays with the children, is no spendthrift . . ." Looking over the list she said, "In a way, I can be glad to have such a husband. Of course, he's quite impossible to live with, but when I see what other husbands are like . . ." Her new attitude provided a basis for the counseling.

PARADOXICAL INTENTION

Paradoxical intention was developed by Frankl in the late twenties and has been adopted, under various names, by other psychotherapies. It makes use of the human capacity for self-distancing in order to break the vicious cycle which traps people who suffer from phobias and obsessive compulsions.

Self-distancing, together with self-transcendence, is the most potent force of the human spirit. It enables us to turn our attention away from ourselves and to open the gates to the outside world. Self-distancing is the capacity to step away from ourselves and to look at ourselves from the "outside," possibly with humor. Self-transcendence is our ability to reach beyond ourselves to people we love or to causes that are important to us.

Both self-distancing and self-transcendence must be mobilized to maintain and restore our health. Every time our sight of the outside world is cut off, we experience an unhealthy introspection, a getting hung up on ourselves. This limits the freedom of our spirit and blocks our growth toward our meaning potentials. An animal sees only itself, but for a human being this is not enough.

Logotherapy uses our capacity for self-distancing in the method of paradoxical intention, and our capacity for self-transcendence in the method of dereflection.

Paradoxical intention is a wish turned upside down. Patients are guided to wish exactly what as phobics and obsessives they have so frantically feared and so desperately tried to avoid. What we flee from tends to catch up with us, and the more we fight a fear the more we become its victims. On the other hand, if we wish to have happen what we fear and support our paradoxical intention with humoristically exaggerated formulations, the fear dissolves.

Example: a students's fear during a test. Excessive anxiety results in a bad grade because it disturbs thinking. Students fail because they fear failure. Paradoxical intention advises them to wish for the worst possible results, to have the firm intention to avoid correct answers. They are to strive for a world record in test-flunking, to find more wrong answers than any student ever before. They cannot take such a paradoxical attitude seriously, they laugh at the idea—and the laughter helps liberate them emotionally so they can concentrate better during the test. The paradoxical intention chases away their fear, and their abilities are no longer blocked. It is not easy to get the students to wish for failure while they fear it. This difficulty can be overcome by the use of their sense of humor which enables them to achieve self-distancing.

Paradoxical intention requires a certain therapeutic skill but is extremely successful as later examples will demonstrate.

An example quoted by Frankl: Mrs. N, 48, was suffering from trembling hands so severely that she could not hold a cup of coffee without spilling. Neither could she write or hold a book firmly enough to read it. During the therapy session Mrs. N. was shaking badly and the counselor decided to try paradoxical intention.

Therapist: Now, Mrs. N, let's have a trembling race.

Mrs. N: What do you mean?

Therapist: We'll see which one of us can tremble faster and longer.

Mrs. N: I didn't know you also suffer from the shakes.

Therapist: I don't, but I can do it if I want to. (He began to tremble fast).

Mrs. N: Oh, you can do it faster than I can. (Smiling, she stepped up her trembling).

Therapist: Faster, Mrs. N, you must do it much faster.

Mrs. N: But I can't! Stop it! I can't keep it up.

She really had become tired. She got up, went to the kitchen, and came back with a cup of coffee. She drank it without spilling a drop. From then on, whenever she began to tremble during a session, all the therapist needed to say was: "How about a race, Mrs. N?" To which she replied laughingly: "All right, all right!" The counselor concluded his report: "It helps every time."

This illustrates how fast paradoxical intention can help in a therapy situation. The question has been raised if such a fast-working cure can have lasting effects. In my experience, paradoxical intention is the most lasting of all methods because patients quickly learn to apply it by themselves in case of a relapse. And I also found that these relapses become less frequent because they are no longer fearfully expected and therefore are no longer triggered by fear.

A few rules have to be observed when applying paradoxical intention. At the beginning of the treatment, the therapist-client contacts must be frequent to be effective. After the first successes the intervals between sessions may become longer because by then patients have learned to apply the method themselves. When they see how their fear loses its grip their cooperation is assured. Relapses occur mostly when the paradoxical formulations are started too late, that is, when the patients are already seized by anticipa-

tory anxiety. As soon as the fear has gripped them and their autonomic nervous system has started to produce the anxiety
symptoms, the patients are unable to wish to have happen what
they fear, and even the humorous formulations cannot achieve
self-distancing. But in the course of my work I have discovered that
even that situation can be rectified.

Case #9

A patient told me that she found paradoxical intention most
effective after a warm bath. When she took a morning bath she was
able, with the help of paradoxical formulations, to remain free of
her phobias for almost the rest of the day. But when she was too
hurried to take her morning bath and came home from her shopping perspiring, the fear would suddenly overwhelm her, before
she could even think of her formulations. She would feel her heart
race and it was impossible for her to wish (paradoxically intending), "it should beat so fast that my whole chest will fly apart,"
because she really believed her last hour had come, and she was
scared stiff.

Her story taught me that relaxing the body through a warm bath
apparently has a positive effect on the application of paradoxical
intention. I suggested to the woman to take a warm bath whenever
she felt seized by fear and to ask a neighbor to be with her, to avoid
her autosuggestion that she would drown while having a heart
attack in the tub. After the bath she should lie down and relax for a
few minutes, and then apply paradoxical intention. This worked
well. Later the patient learned autogenic training, and we replaced
the rather awkward bath in the middle of the day with the warming exercises. After a while she needed neither warming exercises
nor paradoxical intention—she was cured.

This case demonstrated that paradoxical intention could be applied either before the onset of anxiety or during the onset, after a
calming of the patient. The combined paradoxical intention-
autogenic training has proven ideal for treating phobias and obsessive compulsions because it effectively relaxes the patients and
stabilizes the symptoms produced by the autonomic nervous system, even if it is applied after the patients are in the grip of their
symptoms. Paradoxical intention will work *only* when the patients
are relaxed. Any means to achieve relaxation can be used.

DEREFLECTION

Dereflection—using the human capacity of self-transcendence—has proven effective for sleeplessness, sexual dysfunction, addiction, and when problems are caused by excessive self-observation. The aim is to free clients from unhealthy self-reflection by focusing their attention on other interests. Dereflection uses our ability to "forget ourselves" and brings about a therapeutic reordering of attention—turning it from the problem toward other and positive contents of our thinking; it widens and enriches our circle of meaning.

Case #10:

A young man, 16, was deeply unhappy because he suspected himself to be homosexual. After a brief homosexual experience he avoided all human contacts—with men, because he feared a repetition of that unfortunate encounter, and with women, because he was sure he could not relate to them in a positive way. This withdrawal prevented him from having any contact with persons of his own age. He kept more and more to himself and became increasingly shy, unsure of himself, and trapped in self-diagnosis.

I suggested that he pay no special attention to the sex of the people he met and that he see them as individuals who thought, felt, hoped, and lived as he did. To get him away from his frantic sexual reflections and self-observations, I asked him to try, for two weeks, to do something nice to one person every day, regardless of who it was. I was hoping that this would make him, at least temporarily, less self-centered and that he might get positive social feedback from other people, which would help him feel more open toward them.

But the young man resisted. "Why should I be nice to others? They never think of being nice to me," he objected. It was difficult to motivate him and it required many sessions to convince him that he could not expect sympathy, much less love, from others if he was not ready to offer some first. Eventually he agreed to try. I instructed him to take accurate notes of the reactions of others to his small overtures and to report them to me: observing others was to dereflect him from his self-observation. And indeed, he reported eagerly and was happy when someone appreciated his efforts. This way he didn't even notice at first that it was a pretty young girl whom he helped in a sudden cloudburst to open an unmanageable umbrella. They went into a coffeehouse because it rained so hard, and met again another time. Suddenly the young man had "no more time" for therapy sessions; he was busy with his dates. And I don't believe he needed any more therapy because I was sure he didn't think about homosexuality while meeting his new love.

Dereflection can be combined with every kind of reinforcement. When turning *toward* a new interest is successful or is rewarded, turning *from* intense self-observation is more likely to succeed. The essence of dereflection is substituting something positive for something negative. Symptom reduction is only a by-product—but what a by-product!

THE APPEALING TECHNIQUE

The appealing technique rests on the power of suggestion. The question may be raised whether suggestions by therapists contradict the logotherapeutic idea of our free will. And indeed there is a contradiction, and that is why the application of the appealing technique can be justified only when the dimension of the spirit is temporarily blocked. The therapist, using the appealing technique, does what a mother does when a child comes running to her crying and screaming: She first calms the child, and *then* tries to find out what happened. Therapists cannot achieve a modification of attitudes when patients are too excited to listen. They cannot use paradoxical formulations with patients who are near collapse. And they cannot try dereflection with patients who have nothing on their minds but the next drink or the next "fix."

The appealing technique operates in the psychological dimension but opens the way for activating human resources. Because these resources prominently include the will of a person, I have developed a "suggestive training of the will" for patients whose energy level is too weak to carry out any therapy plan requiring their cooperation. The content of the suggestions must stay within what the patients themselves want—or they would not be justified.

In using the appealing technique I never suggest the therapy goal—that's what the patients must reach by themselves when their perception is clear. The freedom to decide must remain theirs.

Some therapists use suggestions after the detoxification of addicts. While the patients are relaxed, their excitement before drug use is simulated, and then certain formulations are suggested, such as, "I don't need any more drugs" or "I'll never again touch a syringe."

This therapy concept is not auspicious because these patients have frequently made similar resolutions themselves and have always failed. They will not expect better results from this therapy, and thus promptly fail again. In my suggestive training of the will no mention is made of drugs or syringes; the therapy goal is not suggested. What is suggested and strengthened is their freedom of will and the defiant power of their spirit, which is entirely in accordance with logotherapeutic concepts. The text is formulated along these lines:

"I am not the helpless victim of my drives and emotions. I have free will and I am going to strengthen my will and reshape my life toward goals that are meaningful to me, toward ideals that are honestly mine. I can feel this inner will; it becomes clearer and clearer, it gives me strength to persist. I shall master my life; master it in spite of all the difficulties. The greater the difficulties the greater my strength will be . . ."

If the counselor firmly assures the patients that they will indeed become stronger, there is a good chance that the patients will be able to act according to their will, even against the temptations of drugs and alcohol. The appealing technique is especially indicated when the patients are unstable, unsure, dependent, young, handicapped, or addicted because such persons tend to be suggestible and also need all the strengthening of their will they can get to make their own decisions and carry them out. The appealing technique can be combined with assertiveness training which also aims at building up a more self-assured and mature personality.

My own experiences and those of other logotherapists have convinced me that the four methods mentioned, or a combination of them, bring about good and lasting results, with relatively few relapses. Today we have sufficient information to know how logotherapy can be integrated in current psychotherapy:

To be applied exclusively where it is indicated and sufficient.

To be applied as a supplement where other methods are indicated but not sufficient.

Research and statistics about logotherapeutic premises and methods have laid a foundation for today's psychotherapy. A foundation is not a complete edifice; it offers support. But research and statistics are not enough. Frankl's greatest contribution to psychotherapy is that he goes beyond statistics, scientific definitions, and hypotheses, calling attention to meanings and values in a time full of doubt and despair. Science has never been able to cure despair and cannot do it in the twentieth century.

Logotherapists are counselors, doctors, and scientists, but also pioneers. They often have to work with methods they themselves have to forge into therapeutic tools. And they may become aware that the most beautiful techniques are not enough, that a grain of human caring weighs more than the most ingenious therapy plan. They will search for the right word at the right time, they will experience setbacks and find new ways. Deep inside they know that they are taking part in a tremendous task: to use the opportunity offered by the crisis of this century to bring about the rehumanization of psychotherapy.

4

The Application of Modification of Attitudes

Our fourth premise warned that psychotherapy must not disregard any of the three dimensions; it must deal with the total person. Yet how difficult this is in practice! Patients come and seek help, sick perhaps in body, perhaps in psychological functioning, perhaps in self-interpretation. Every dimension affects the others, everything is interwoven in the tapestry that makes up the person, a tangled net of interactions and biofeedback mechanisms. No therapist can hope to set up a plan that will fully reach all of a patient's dimensions, consider all possible feedback reactions, grasp—and cure—the total person.

I want to begin this chapter with a warning: Therapists must watch out that, while helping their clients in one dimension, they do not harm them in another. The following example illustrates what can happen if the close interrelationship among the dimensions is not sufficiently taken into consideration.

Case #11

A 53 year-old woman had been referred to me by her physician because of severe attacks of psychosomatic spasms and paralysis. For three years she had fought an alimony suit against her ex-husband who, although well-off, refused to pay anything toward her living expenses. He argued that she could earn a living now that the children were independent. The woman claimed that at her age, and untrained for any job, she could not find work. The judge at the superior court took pity on the helpless woman. He ordered a physician from the Public Health Department to give her a thorough examination, and to list all the deteriorations of her health he could find in order to provide the judge with arguments why the woman was unable to work an eight-hour day.

The judge meant well, but he took only one level of the woman's life into account—her economic situation. Any feedback process into the dimensions of her spirit remained unconsidered.

The woman had felt quite well and had not taken the medical examination too seriously. Suddenly she heard from the medical opinion, as it was read in court, that her heart muscle was damaged, her blood pressure was high, that she had a curvature of the spine, that her bone structure was irregular, and her thyroid gland enlarged. All this was expressed in a string of—to her—ominous-sounding Latin terms which panicked her because she could not understand them. The shock caused a spasm in her diaphragm, she suffered an attack of psychogenic choking, and collapsed in the courtroom. The physician who was summoned quickly could, of course, not see through the connections and prescribed, instead of tranquilizers, some stimulating injections which caused further spasms so that the woman had to be taken to the hospital by ambulance.

She finally won the court case, but was sick for many months. She consulted various physicians and was finally referred to our clinic.

It took some time to clarify the origin of her condition, but then she was free of her symptoms within a few weeks by a combination of psychopharmaceutics, autogenic training, and paradoxical intention.

Occasionally, physicians, too, act like the judge. They mean well, but pay attention only to one, the physical, dimension of the patient. By disregarding the effects on the other dimensions they may say things that cause anxiety and worry in their patients and trigger an unnecessary "iatrogenic" (physician-caused) neurosis.

Psychologists, too, may cause damage to their clients by telling them, without considering the consequences, the data of test results. And the warning is also pertinent for teachers and parents. I have often heard it said about a child that has failed, "We have always known he couldn't do it" or "We never expected anything better," and I cannot help suspecting that this "always having known" or the "never having expected anything else" contributed prominently to the child's failure. If children repeatedly hear that they are too stupid, too slow, or too lazy for this or that, these judgments penetrate deep into their self-understanding and steer their development in a negative direction. The power of suggestion and feedback mechanisms have undoubtedly a stronger influence than we realize.

Interactions among the three dimensions are not only a hazard for physicians, psychologists, and educators, but provide a tremendous opportunity. Logotherapy makes use of this opportunity.

Logotherapists may not be able to grasp the fullness of the human being in its totality, but it is possible to treat clients in their diversity. Medical treatments such as surgery, medication, X-ray and chemotherapy remain in the biological dimension. Techniques such as psychoanalysis, behavior or Gestalt therapy act on a psychological level. Logotherapy, however, dares to enter the dimension of the spirit, an area that for centuries had been left to religion. Today, many people feel too uncomfortable to turn to clergymen with their human problems and succumb to an existential vacuum. A high standard of living and a fat bank account cannot, in the long run, fill inner emptiness. Traditional values that have crumbled cannot be glued together again, and current philosophies of life, shaped by two world wars, lend little support.

Logotherapy, drawing on the resources of the human spirit, fills this void—not so much on a philosophical, and certainly not on a theological basis, but on medical grounds. It places meaning at the center of our search because it is healthy. But by going beyond the biological-psychological dimension, logotherapy leaves the secure area of things that can be systematized and catalogued, of what can be intellectually taught and learned. It even foregoes, at least in part, the methodologies of definite psychotechniques, to make room for the simple humanity of the patients.

To go back to the metaphor of the piano concert, a discord may have several reasons: the piano may be out of tune, the pianist may have hit the wrong keys, or the composition itself may be at fault. Obviously the discord cannot always be corrected by the same method. The piano may have to be tuned, the pianist may have to practice more, or the composition may have to be rewritten. The comparison with the discords in human health is flawed, yes—but it makes the point: Just as tuning the piano will not improve a faulty composition, so a mechanistic psychotechnique will not cure a noogenic depression. Neither is logotherapy a cure-all. But together with other therapies, it presents a decisive step toward human health.

A modification of attitudes is an important step in the logotherapy program, especially when clients find themselves in situations that are void of meaning yet cannot be changed—"blows of fate," accidents, incurable disease, the irrevocable ending of a relationship, a career, a life. It is possible and therapeutic to find a meaningful attitude toward a situation which in itself is meaningless.

Modification is also therapeutic for attitudes that are negative, destructive, or reductionistic. The therapist does not decide whether an attitude is "correct" or "moral," but whether it is healthy. Often, common sense serves as a guideline.

During the initial therapy session, the clients are not likely to reveal their basic attitudes toward life—their desires, aims, and hopes. First, a basic trust must be established.

When this stage has been reached and the clients' attitudes have come into the open, the therapist must decide objectively and nonjudgmentally which attitudes are psychohygienically unhealthy and a "psychological burden," and which attitudes can be considered healthy and have a positive influence on the clients' life and even survival. Obviously it is not up to the therapist to decide what are "good" or "bad" attitudes. Yet certain attitudes are undeniably the causes or expressions of an unhappy, self-destructive life.

Negative attitudes are indicated in remarks like these: "There's no point in my trying, things always go wrong with me," or "I don't want to have anything to do with people, they are all beasts." An unhealthy attitude may be suspected when a mother says: "I've got to take care of my children, or the juvenile courts will breathe down my neck," or if a wife declares, "My husband and I live our own lives, but that's all right, no one interferes with the other." Therapists cannot "prescribe" different attitudes but must be able to tune in on the underlying message. If an unhealthy attitude is apparent, the therapist dares to question it and help the clients see that they have other choices.

Research has shown the psychosomatic connection between attitude and the body's reaction to it. We have statistical evidence that men devoted to their work or mothers with small children tend to be immune to flu epidemics: they simply "have no time" to be sick because they feel needed. Equally well-known is the observation that sick persons who give up are in danger.

The body is affected by fear as well as by depression, by joy as well as by love and happiness. No physician can afford to say: "What this patient feels inside doesn't concern me, that's his affair. I take care of his appendix, or her kidney attack, or his cancer." Psychotherapists, too, must watch out for dangerous, unhealthy attitudes; must challenge and argue in favor of a more positive attitude.

A modification of attitudes may not always succeed but must be attempted. Sometimes a remnant of the healthy argumentation is left in the unconscious mind of the client and emerges during an acute crisis situation.

Case #12:

Steve had a severe and incurable speech defect. He avoided young women because he was afraid they would laugh at him. All my attempts at changing his attitude failed. I suggested that women who made fun of him were not mature enough to make good partners, but he said he didn't give a damn about their maturity, he just wanted to dance and have fun like his friends. I challenged him to go to a discotheque where the noise would drown out his speech defect, and I argued that "the worth of a person does not depend on how well one speaks," but he rejected this too. We discussed other ideas such as making friends with a woman who was in some way handicapped herself. But he refused "to take what no one else wanted."

His self-defeating attitude gradually extended to other areas and blocked all therapeutic cooperation. We decided to interrupt the counseling for half a year. Before that time was up, I received an urgent call from a clinic. Steve had been brought in after a suicide attempt and had asked for me.

After some drinks, and alone in his apartment, Steve had cut his artery. Seeing his blood gush out, he had apparently sobered up enough to call emergency. When the doctor arrived in his apartment, Steve was barely conscious and repeated over and over again: "The worth . . . of a person . . . does not depend . . . on how one speaks."

My logotherapeutic argumentation which he had rejected months ago, had proven stronger in the decisive moment of a crisis than his despair and resignation.

The case touched me deeply. Steve had matured through his experience. He had struggled with himself and ultimately said "yes" to life. He stuck to his decision. After this incident he was open to the Socratic dialogue without the constant resistance of a "yes-but" attitude.

Therapists are here not to judge whether an attitude is good or bad but to use their knowledge, experience and intuition to decide when a client in a certain situation is displaying an attitude that is harmful, unhealthy, or possibly dangerous and destructive. The logotherapist is on guard as soon as the dialogue reveals attitudes of negative determinism, and does not shy away from openly discussing them. Here she goes beyond the client-oriented counselor who helps the client see himself through mirroring. She goes far beyond the behavior therapist who disregards subjective variables as much as possible and concentrates on quantifiable reaction patterns. And she goes in the direction opposite to that of a psychoanalyst who uncovers psychological repressions without paying attention to attitudes or cognitive feedback reactions.

Case # 13:

But cognitive feedback reactions cannot be ignored, and they often manifest themselves in physical symptoms. These connections were apparent in the case of 21-year-old Inge who was sent to me by an abortion clinic for a routine psychological authorization. Inge came to me with drooping shoulders, lowered eyes, feet dragging. She hardly dared to take off her coat, finally sat down on the edge of a chair, and began to stammer, her perspiring hands in constant motion. She wanted the abortion because bringing up a child was beyond her; she felt insecure and afraid of the future.

I listened patiently. I wanted her to relax and learn to trust me. I turned on the soft light of a floor lamp and took no notes to avoid irritating her. Gradually she lifted her head, made eye contact occasionally, and spoke more fluently. After half an hour she made a statement to which I have become highly allergic because it betrays an unhealthy, deterministic attitude. "My parents never let me take care of my own affairs. They always made the decisions for me, and now that I am grown-up I don't know what to do. They still see me as a little girl, and I have always followed their advice. And now I cannot make up my mind because no one tells me what to do. It's all my parents' fault."

This is a widely held unhealthy attitude. Of course, it was possible that her parents dominated and protected her too much. But if she now, as a grown woman, could not free herself from this dependency, if she considered herself hopelessly incapable of making her own decisions, if she saw no chance to liberate herself from her childlike attitude, then she *had* no chance. She was stuck and would not be much more mature at the age of 50 because her fixed attitude had choked off her maturing. And the physical symptoms were the telltale signs: the lowered eyes, the perspiring hands, the erratic movements; this entire hyperneurotic reaction pattern was the result of her unhealthy attitude.

This, then, was the critical point when I could no longer listen passively, when I felt challenged to open her eyes in a Socratic dialogue along the following lines: "You claim your upbringing made you dependent and helpless. Do you want us to use our time together to support this dependency and helplessness, so they influence your life more and more? If you wish, we can talk about your dependency, we can look for its roots, and you will become increasingly aware of your helplessness the more clearly you see the causes. You may decide to have the abortion which will confirm your conviction that you are not able to master the tasks of your life, that you are indeed a failure. I wonder what your life will be like if you keep avoiding the difficult tasks because you feel you can't handle them?"

Inge sat a long time, thinking. "I don't want to be a failure forever," she finally said. "What shall I do?"

We talked for two more hours, without perspiring hands and without lowered eyes. "Why did your parents overprotect you?" I asked her, and she had to admit that it was because they loved her. "If you were raised by parents who loved you," I said, "then you have a good basis for your own behavior. You, too, can love, and love is the first thing your baby will need if you decide to have it. The next thing you need is the strength to take responsibility—for yourself and for those in your care. You cannot blame your unwillingness to take on responsibility on your childhood or your parents, without a feeling of discomfort and failure. Every time you do make a responsible decision, your capacity is strengthened to carry it out. If you make an 'easy' decision because it seems most comfortable at the moment, it will weigh on you later on." In this vein I tried to mobilize Inge's resources of the human spirit and fortify her self-confidence. In the end I handed her the certificate authorizing the abortion and placed the decision in her hands.

A few days later she returned and said she had thought everything over and decided to have the baby. For the next three months I gave her some assertiveness training, and this was followed by a discussion of her future plans. When we concluded the counseling, her attitude toward life had changed; she was serene, confident, and looked forward to having her child.

The "bad-parents complex" often lies behind unhealthy attitudes. For years psychologists have been looking for mistakes made by parents. Parents have been blamed for being too authoritarian, too indifferent, too critical, too success-oriented, not democratic enough, too unsure, too inconsistent—until many parents indeed became unsure of themselves and for that reason alone made mistakes. Contributing factors were the crumbling of traditions and the bulk of contradictory pedagogic literature. Parents have become the favorite target for their children's failures, and it is no wonder that young people themselves all too readily point the finger at their parents to explain their own weaknesses.

Undoubtedly parents do make mistakes in bringing up their children. Also, the increasing numbers of working mothers cause an additional strain on the family. But a large percentage of parents lovingly care for their children, endure sacrifices, and do their best to prepare them for the future. Their affectionate concern cannot be simply swept aside while paying attention only to those moments when they lose their nerve or fail to find the right word at the right moment.

True, it has been proven that clients are helped when they see connections between their development and their upbringing. But it has been proven as well that such a looking back may set in motion a feedback process that reduces their sense of responsibility for their actions. They are prone to say: "I cannot act differently; this the the way I have been shaped," and this attitude blocks the path to further growth and maturity. Ego strengthening is not enough. What is needed is a vital process of self-discovery, not only in terms of who they are, but also in terms of who they can still become. And this process requires recognition of their own responsibility.

Admittedly, each person is equipped from the start with different gifts, some amply, others poorly. But whatever the base, the young must build on it. A part of their success is up to them alone; they can fail in spite of rich natural gifts, and they can succeed in spite of poor ones. Young people have to be made aware that their course is not set once and for all, that they can give their lives a direction toward the positive as well as the negative.

Sometimes the therapist has no parental base on which to build. The young patients have nothing but negative childhood influences, they have many "excuses" for failure, but even they have the defiant power *not* to fail, in spite of everything.

Case #14:

This young girl never knew her father. Neither her mother nor her grandparents had shown any interest in her. She was raised in an orphanage, flunked out of school when she was thirteen, and was fired from three apprenticeships because she was so afraid of failure that she pretended to have pains and fainting spells. After that she found no more apprenticeships, began to lie, led the life of a tramp, drifted into a dream world, and was in danger of becoming a prostitute. Our talks which had been initiated by the head of the orphanage showed no progress either. I tried in vain to show her how to take responsibility for her own life. I suggested ways to find a way back to a more satisfying life pattern, and we practiced the method of paradoxical intention (see next chapter) and logo-drama to overcome the anxieties that gripped her when starting a new apprenticeship.

During my summer vacation she got into bad company and I did not hear from her. Half a year later I received a letter from which I quote—not to show the belated fruits of my efforts, but to give evidence that a human being has the power to turn her life, by her own efforts, from a seemingly hopeless situation into a positive direction.

"Dear Dr. Lukas," she wrote. "I'm sorry I have not written to you for so long. Please forgive me. I have to tell you so many things. I called you at your office but I was told you were out. I'd like to see you again. I can come only on Thursdays—that's my day off. I have a cool job, I feel good there, I'm happy to work there. Dear Dr. Lukas, now I really found the right thing for me. Yes, I did it! I have worked here for three months and am very proud about it.

"You told me a good trick which I tried when I was in the dumps. It helped. I really am grateful. Dear Dr. Lukas, I like you very much. I believe I can trust you more than I trust anyone. Please believe me. The talisman you gave me I always have with me at work. It helps me every time I need it. Dear Dr. Lukas, I have a big request, please don't think I'm mushy. I'd like a snapshot of yourself. As a souvenir. It would make me very happy. And I hope I can come to see you and talk . . ."

The "talisman" she mentioned was a coin I had given her with the advice to look at it whenever she was in trouble. And the "trick" was paradoxical intention and logodrama. We practiced how she would behave when applying for an apprenticeship. Before her anxiety set in she was, paradoxically, to intend to make the worst possible impression, not to comprehend anything, and to do everything wrong so she would "get fired before she was even hired." No one could laugh about these paradoxical logodramas more heartily than this young girl, and although we broke off our therapy before she could practice it, I had been convinced that her sense of humor would bring it off successfully when she was ready.

What enabled her to change her attitudes and her life was not a psychotherapeutic trick but a mutual relationship which she once expressed by saying, "I wish you were my mother!" But what speaks in her letter is not a "transference" in the traditional analytical sense. It is a genuine feeling of affection which she had never experienced at home or at the orphanage. That she was able to experience such an affection is amazing. That she was able, in addition, to have the will to change and succeed, is a truly human achievement.

Perhaps she will not completely succeed in every respect after her new beginning but she knows the way and her ability to walk it.

THE UNWANTED ADULT

Psychotherapy can explain human failure but must not serve to excuse it. An unhappy life may be the consequence of an unhappy childhood, but is not its inevitable result. An unwanted child is not destined to become an unwanted adult. An honest poll probably would show that a large percentage of children were not truly wanted or planned by both their parents. Can we assume that these children were secretly loved less because they were not fervently desired during pregnancy? Can a parent's love not grow during that time? Can a mother not accept her child with joy even if she had doubts before its birth? It is risky for a mother to admit to a psychologist that the child was originally not planned or wanted. He may be inclined to condemn her however she treats the child. If she is cool and controlled in its upbringing, he might say she rejects the child because it was unwanted. If she is warm and caring, he might suspect that she unconsciously hates the child and overcompensates to hide her repressed feelings. Whatever the mother (or the father) does, the child cannot develop to perfection, at least not in the opinion of psychologists with such an orientation.

Suppose the mother conceived the child against her will and deep inside really rejects it. And suppose further that as compensation she is especially loving to the child. This has to be acknowledged as a grandiose achievement by the mother who does not want the child to know that it was born against her wishes. The mother takes a stand against her own inner rejection of the child, to spare the child suffering. There is heroism in such a stand. One becomes a mother not by anticipating a child with great joy but mostly by loving a child in spite of all difficulties. It is destructive reductionism to say that the achievement of such mother-love is "nothing but" a compensation for an inner aggressive drive.

Case #15:

Mrs A. came to me because of difficulties with her teenage daughter Janie. When Janie was a child, Mrs. A had played and exercised with her. Doing a somersault, Janie had hurt her spine and suffered pain for many years. After extensive treatments Janie was completely well but Mrs A. had developed a phobia about her. She could not bear to see the girl ride a bike, and broke out in a sweat when Janie came home from school a few minutes late. Her husband and Janie laughed about her fears, and Janie became completely unmanageable.

Mrs. A had been in psychoanalysis for almost two years but her phobia had not lessened. When she had asked the therapist to help her with her problems with Janie, he had replied that he did not deal with problems of child-rearing and so she had turned to our counseling center. Sadly she said: "He never helped me with Janie. He kept asking me about my childhood. For hours I had to tell him about the past. When I asked him what to do about Janie, he said that I had to know that myself, and when I would no longer be sick I would know. That meant to me that I am still sick because I often don't know what to do about Janie. I don't have the money for therapy twice a week, and so I resigned myself to being not quite normal. But I don't want to do more harm to my child, and so I ask you to tell me what I have done wrong in raising Janie."

I first explained to Mrs. A that we could not separate her "sickness" and her pedagogical problems because both were triggered by her excessive anxiety about Janie. But she need not accept her anxiety as permanent; it was not her "normal" condition but rather the result of the unfortunate accident. Just as Janie had physically overcome the accident, so Mrs. A could overcome it psychologically.

Paradoxical intention which ordinarily is helpful for phobias could not be used in this case because it was difficult to find formulations the mother could be expected to intend paradoxically (as, for instance, "I wish Janie would hurt herself badly"). I therefore worked exclusively with a modification of attitudes. I told Mrs. A that although she was terribly worried about Janie's health she did not need to *act* according to her worried state. She was free in her actions and also could take a stand against her anxiety. She could decide to let her daughter go bicycling and at home suffer from her worries while telling herself: "I sent her bicycling in spite of my anxiety!" And—an important point—she could be proud of her action because to "boycott" her anxiety is an achievement, all the more so the greater the anxiety. She could point out to her husband and daughter that she had made her decision in spite of her neurosis, which they would have to acknowledge—there was no more cause for ridicule. I also tried to appeal to her mother-love by saying that children learn from the example of their parents, and there was the danger that Janie might transfer the anxiety she saw in her mother to her own future behavior patterns. It might make a difference in Janie's life to see that anxiety need not immobilize people, but that one can act sensibly in spite of strong emotions.

Mrs. A was receptive to my arguments, and after several sessions herself suggested the following: Janie's greatest wish was to learn to ride a horse, but Mrs. A had violently objected although her husband sided with Janie. Now she had decided to surprise her daughter and drive her to a riding school to inquire about the conditions. She said: "I know I'll be sick at the thought of Janie sitting on a horse which could run away and throw her off. And I won't pretend to Janie that I'll feel all right about it, but she should know that my love for her is stronger than my fear. But I have a question that has been on my mind for a long time. You see, my psychiatrist interpreted my fears about Janie as a deep-seated and repressed wish for Janie's death. All my fears, he said, were a symbol of an inner aggression toward Janie. And this thought depressed me more than my sickness, it's so terrible! Is it possible that deep inside I really hate my child, that this is the reason I caused her injury? Am I really so evil? O Lord, can it be true?"

Such situations always present a dilemma for me because to contradict another therapist undermines the client's trust toward all. But in this case it was absolutely necessary to sweep away all doubts about her motherly feelings, and to strengthen her trust in herself. Instead of curing a phobia, the therapist had added an iatrogenic neurosis which I tried to counteract with positive-oriented arguments:

"I am certainly not all-knowing and cannot see what goes on in the depth of your unconscious, but the one thing I have heard from all your words is your genuine affection for your family, and especially for your daughter. Your playing and exercising with your daughter a few years ago was done out of love. The accident was truly that—an accident. Janie could have hurt her spine just playing in a playground. Your suffering and worries afterwards are also proof of how much you love Janie. Hate is not the opposite of love. Indifference is. And nobody will be able to convince you that you are indifferent to Janie. But the greatest proof of your love was your suggestion today to drive Janie to a riding school. Only someone who knows the tortures of the human soul will be able to appreciate what the suggestion meant to you; it is the victory of love over your fear! No further proofs are necessary for you to know that my colleague was mistaken; his mistake is as obvious as your love for Janie. You must not be too harsh on psychology for making mistakes. It is a young science. When the natural sciences were as young as psychology is today, scientists still were convinced that the earth was a disk floating on the ocean and that Apollo was driving across·the sky on a chariot . . ."

At that, Mrs. A broke into a relieved laugh and declared happily that she would bury the thought of hating Janie for all times—she never really was able to believe it.

Janie received her riding lessons, and Mrs. A was able to reduce a large part of her fears. Their relationship improved as I explained to Janie what it had meant for her mother to overcome her fears and let Janie lead a normal and healthy life. The youngster appreciated her mother's self-control, and what was equally important, Mr. A began to believe once more in his wife's gradual recovery and supported her in her efforts. From time to time Mrs. A suffers from attacks of anxiety, but she can handle them and is increasingly confident that they will improve because she herself now can believe in her eventual recovery.

DISTANCING FROM SYMPTOMS

Modification of attitudes is the second of four steps in the logotherapeutic treatment plan. The sequence of this plan may be changed as the situation requires. Ordinarily, this first step, distancing, prepares the patients to gain distance from their symptoms, to become more objective. This is followed by a modification of attitudes which leads to the third step—a reduction of symptoms. When symptoms are reduced, even vanish, or at least become bearable, the patients are open to the fourth step in the logotherapeutic treatment: an orientation toward meaningful activities and experiences.

As long as clients identify with their symptoms, it is difficult for them to gain new self-understanding. As long as they see themselves as sick, they *are* sick. If they consider help impossible, help *is* impossible. If they think of themselves as the victims of their childhood experiences, they *are* victims. Obsessive compulsive patients really believe they are under a compulsion, phobics really see themselves as excessively in danger, stutterers are certain they are not able to speak fluently, sexual neurotics really see themselves as impotent, failing students really consider themselves stupid, depressive patients really believe they are destined to be sad, and patients suffering from paranoia really are convinced they are being attacked and observed.

As long as these clients see themselves as closely tied to their symptoms, the symptoms will have them in their grip. And the close tie between client and symptom is rooted in unhealthy attitudes and hypotheses held by the client.

The therapist, having gained the trust of the clients, must as a first step fight the identification of the clients with their symptoms. They must be prevented from believing in their unhealthy hypothesis, or they will get so fixated in it that self-distancing becomes more and more difficult.

Case #16:

The therapist seeks first to combat the identification of a patient with the symptoms presented. Mrs. P came to the center because she was, as she stated, unable to respond sexually to her second husband due to the brutal treatment she had received from her first husband. As long as she was in the grip of her own hypothesis, as long as she said, "I am frigid, I am unable to love because . . ." no cure was likely because nothing could be done to change what had happened between her and her first husband. She was enmeshed in her dependency, felt determined by her trauma, and identified with her symptom.

It was my task to liberate her from her unfortunate hypothesis that she *was* frigid, and to show her that she was a woman who *had* a problem with frigidity, that frigidity was something she had acquired and again could get rid of. My arguments went like this: "The experience with your first husband is no reason why you cannot love your second one. There is no connection between these two men, they are different people, meeting you at different times of your life. You yourself are not the same person you were during your first marriage. You love your present husband and want to give him your love, otherwise you wouldn't have come to me. It is an unfortunate experience, a bad memory that fills your head and causes all sorts of mischief. In reality you are able to love your husband with all your heart, with all your will, with your whole person. We won't empower that unfortunate memory, we won't let it destroy your happiness. If that memory turns up again, speak to it. Tell it: 'Oh, it's you again? Well, I know you well enough by now; you are no longer as interesting to me as you once were. Why don't you go back where you came from; namely, to the past where you belong? I now have more important things to do than worry about you.' If you think along these lines, the hold of old memories will weaken and your inner strength will become free so you can turn your attention to your present happy situation."

This is essential in the logotherapeutic process: patients are encouraged to speak freely about their innermost hopes and fears, but when they voice harmful explanations which they have pieced together, the time for logotherapeutic action has come. Dependencies have to be loosened, even when the therapist can well understand them. Only after the clients have been liberated from their pathogenic hypothesis of dependency can they turn to a new and healthy attitude that can counteract their symptoms. They must be freed from the grip of their psychological illness, a distance must be placed between the self and the symptoms. Never again the declaration: "I *am* fearful." Instead, they go on to say: "Here I am, well and normal—and over there is a ridiculous fear that sometimes wants to grab me, but I'll show this fear who is master!" The defiant power of the human spirit is aroused to bring about the necessary self-distancing.

THE SEARCH FOR HEALTHY ATTITUDES

The liberation of the clients from their belief in a dependency brings enormous relief. Phobics who realize that they are not the hopeless victims of their fears and can even laugh about them, and young adults who realize that parental overprotection does not prevent them from taking charge of their life, are ready for the second step in their treatment: the search for a new and healthier attitude.

An attitude is healthy if it directs clients toward goals that are meaningful for them, or at least keeps the path open toward such goals. An attitude is unhealthy if it promotes an existential frustration (as in the case of Steve who avoided women because of his speech defect) or if it undermines the will to make decisions (as in the case of the girl who believed her upbringing had weakened her ability to take charge of her life).

Ordinarily, the modification of attitudes follows directly upon the distancing of patient from symptoms. In the case of Mrs. P, for instance, I led her to see that her unfortunate experiences in her first marriage had positive potentials because they could help her appreciate her happiness in her second marriage more intensively. I talked to her, during the next several sessions, along these lines: "Just *because* you have gone through marital suffering in the past you can now appreciate your present husband and be a much better wife than many others who jeopardize their marriage frivolously with petty quarrels because they do not know yet how brutal an unhappy union can be." I tried to effect a change in attitude from "I no longer can truly love" to the attitude of "I can love my husband all the more because I already know a different version of marriage." Once this change in attitude had occurred, Mrs. P became sexually responsive. She had gained a new understanding of herself and of her capacity to love her husband for an added reason, and this enabled her to overcome her physical block as a natural outcome of the depth of her feelings for him. We reached the third step—the reduction of symptoms, although the symptoms had not been treated directly.

Thomas Edison is quoted as saying: "That's the beauty in making a mistake, because you do not have to make it a second time." Implied in this sentence is the possibility to decide freely in spite of all the mistakes one has made because of genetic make-up, faulty learning and social influences. The logotherapist guides the client toward an attitude of "I don't have to." Even if I have made a mistake twenty times, I don't have to make it a twenty-first time. Even if a psychological disturbance has taken place every day, it doesn't have to take place tomorrow. Undoubtedly, every failure increases the probability for further failures, and yet there remains

the chance that a person finds enough strength to defy this probability. This "you don't have to" is the "therapeutic credo" of
logotherapy that is transmitted to the client.

Case #17:

Peter, 18 years old, was referred to our counseling center by the
juvenile court. He was the illegitimate child of a woman who had
ten other children from various fathers. Peter was raised by a number of relatives and foster parents in vastly differing styles, had
never known continuity, security, and daily routines. Drunken
and violent men made their appearance, and often the child was
snatched out of bed in the middle of the night and hidden in a
cellar where he sometimes was "forgotten" for a while. Finally he
found foster parents who tried their best, but had great trouble
with him. They compared his erratic behavior and poor performance in school with those of their own children. Twice he ran
away, got caught for minor offenses like shoplifting, damaging
property, stealing bicycles. After he failed in three jobs, his foster
parents repudiated him, and from then on he went downhill. By
the time he came to me he had quit or been fired from thirteen jobs,
and he was depressed and rebellious, convinced he was not able to
hold any job.

All this background was contained in a thick file the juvenile
court had sent me with the request to decide what chances I still
could see for Peter. The facts contained in the file would have
justified the judgment that there was no hope. Nevertheless, I
challenged the young man. I told him that his record justified the
doubt that he could straighten out, and even he himself had given
up. But, I added, I was not prepared to give him up. I would close
the file in front of his eyes and would forget everything I had read
in it. We would start all over again, as if all the opportunities of life
were still going to be open to him. He had never learned con-
stancy, reliability, or endurance in his childhood, so it was time to
learn them by himself. He would learn these qualities out of his
own experiences, and his failures were the "tuition" he had to pay
for life's lessons. Other people learn from education or the example
of their parents; he would learn from ten or twenty unsuccessful
attempts. When ready to graduate from this "education through

failures" school, he would value the importance of sticking it out and "enter life" as any other graduate. He would have to put out a serious effort to make a new start and this time he would succeed.

Peter listened with interest because this was the first time someone expressed confidence in him and expected him to succeed. He started as a helper in a toy store, with good intentions, but was too clumsy and lost his job. That was his fourteenth attempt. After the seventeenth he was ready to give up and, only after great effort, was I able to persuade him to try once more. He had to unload cars for a florist, deliver flowers, and occasionally was allowed to help with gardening. One year later he is still there and was given the opportunity to become an apprentice. He is proud of his achievement and goes to an evening school to make up for some of his missed high-school courses. To vary Edison's statement: "That's the beauty in making a mistake, because you do not have to repeat it eighteen times!"

Case #18:

In cases of what Frankl has called the "tragic triad" (unavoidable suffering, inerasable guilt, and death) it is not possible to attain the first and third steps of logotherapy procedure. No one can attain distance from the "symptoms" of suffering, guilt and death, nor can these be eliminated. In such cases the other two steps, modification of attitudes and orientation toward meaning, are all the more important.

Mrs. M was desperate because her eight-year-old son Walter was so hypersensitive to pain that it was impossible to live with him. When his baby tooth was loose he could not brush his teeth; when his bath was a trifle cold he could not stay in; the smallest scratch became a tragedy. A medical examination showed that Walter was suffering from dermographia, a somatically conditioned oversensitivity which might improve in later years but had to be accepted at least during his childhood. To find a starting point for a modification of attitudes (without hope of changing the symptoms), I explored the daily routine of the child, and discovered that Walter was unusually musical, was praised by his music teacher for his absolute pitch, and had even participated in concerts. The mother was proud of his talent.

Here was the opportunity to try a modification of attitudes. I led Mrs. M to perceive that life had offered an alternative for Walter: either absolute pitch requiring a delicate acoustic sensitivity but also a similarly delicate sensitivity in other areas, or no such musical talents, no musical ear but also no sensitivity; instead, a robust stability. Mrs. M could perceive her son's sensitivity to pain as a price he had to pay for being a musical genius. She even found a healthy way to handle Walter's sensitivity. Whenever he cried about minor pains she started to sing and asked him to sing along and thus "dereflected" him toward something positive. This also reduced her anger at Walter's oversensitivity because her new attitude allowed her to concentrate on some positive aspects in her child.

Case #19:

The following case illustrates how a modification of attitudes was achieved in an emergency situation, and also how an unfortunate coincidence can become the "logohook" for finding a treatment plan which up to then had eluded discovery.

Hilde M, 55, suffered from endogenous depressions which had started several years earlier, after one of her daughters had been in a car accident and died seven weeks later without ever regaining consciousness. The other three children had grown up and moved away, and Hilde felt useless.

One day she called me in utter despair and confusion. I could not understand her stammering and I asked her to come to see me immediately.

Trembling and choking with tears she told me the following: Today was her birthday. None of her children was with her and she had gone to her mailbox to see if anyone had remembered her. She found only one letter, addressed to her dead child, sent from the hospital where her daughter had died. Mrs. M considered it "a mockery of fate" that this letter had reached her on her birthday, to remind her of her tragedy. She was in shock, completely devastated, and I put her down on a couch, trying to calm her.

Eventually I took the unopened letter from her perspiring hands and found it a routine request by a young doctor working on a dissertation about collarbone fractures. He had seen from the hospital files that Mrs. M's daughter had suffered such a fracture, and failed to notice that she had died. The letter contained questions about the consequences of the fracture. But my explanations only upset Mrs. M even more. She said that God Himself must have wanted to punish her by letting this letter show up in her mailbox on her birthday. This interpretation encouraged me to try for a modification of attitudes along her own way of thinking. "God may have intervened, as you suggest, but in a different way than you think. Isn't it possible that He has chosen this way for you to receive a greeting from your dead daughter? We'll send back the letter with an explanation, but you keep the envelope. Your daughter's name is on it, and it came on your birthday. It's like a birthday wish. Your other three children live their own lives, they hardly have time for their mother's birthday, but this child has no opportunity to congratulate her mother. Through this coincidence she has come alive again in your thoughts and your heart. Isn't it like a miracle? I don't think that fate wanted to torment you through this mistake of the doctor—you have suffered enough. Perhaps fate wanted to comfort you by playing this memory into your hands, just on your birthday—it's like a gentle greeting from your daughter. . . ."

Mrs. M sat very quietly for a long time. Then she placed the envelope carefully into her handbag, stood up, pressed my hand, and left.

Somehow she was now able to bear her pain because the misdirected letter had taken on a meaning which was acceptable to her within her expressed values. The unhealthy attitude, her belief that everything had conspired against her, had given way to the perception of a symbol of daughterly love that had reached her from beyond the grave.

To the well-known saying, "Every crisis has its opportunity" could be added another one: "Every suffering has it meaning." The meaning does not lie in the suffering itself but can be attained by one's attitude toward it. It is not easy to find a meaningful attitude toward a suffering which in itself is meaningless, but if the therapist succeeds in helping the client find it, she can be certain that the client will not be destroyed by the suffering.

Case #20:

A young woman sought help with these desperate words: "Nobody wants me. I don't want to live any more!" The reason: Her face was cruelly marred by a car accident, and her husband left her.

We struggled for a long time to find a new attitude that would enable her to want to go on living. The first smile crossed her lips, the beginning of a new hope, when I offered her the following consideration: "Maybe the blow of fate that made you lose your outer beauty has also given you a precise measuring instrument. Whenever you meet new people you can test them to see if they have the character to become genuine friends, or if they only go by superficial things and appearances. You have something like a Geiger counter that can help you spot, not valuable metals, but valuable people. Your husband has not passed the test. Your outer defect was not at fault. His inner defect which you could not see so clearly without your misfortune was at fault. If you will be looking for a new partner and will have to wait longer than others, your time will not be wasted with false friendships. Others don't have such an instrument that tells them if they are appreciated for their own sake. You will be able to recognize true friendship from people who really like you and will not exclude you because of your looks but who admire you for your courage. There may not be too many genuinely valuable people around but their number would not be larger if you had the looks of a movie star—only they would then fool you. Your suffering has given you the means to distinguish human chaff from human wheat, and that can be more desirable than the most handsome face which will fade with age."

The smile that came over her deformed features was the first sign of a new courage to live. From that moment on she slowly improved, and a few months later she again dared to go on hikes with friends and seek their company as other young people do.

The logotherapeutic modification of attitudes differs from most patient-centered psychotechniques in which the therapist remains relatively passive and, by quiet listening, understanding, or mirroring, creates situations that will encourage the clients to reveal themselves. The logotherapist actively participates in the dialogue and even offers healthy opposition where necessary. She will say "no" to the oppressive compulsive: "No, you will *not* do what you are afraid of, your very fear guarantees that." She will say "no" to the depressed patient: "No, it is *not* true that your life has no meaning, and I'll help you find it." An expression of understanding or a mirroring may enmesh the client into his problem more deeply. If a client states that he no longer enjoys his life, a logotherapist will not say: "I understand that very well after all you have gone through" (understanding), or "You mean you don't want to go on living, you want to die?" (mirroring), but she will say: "And what about the tasks, out there in life, that are still waiting for you?"

Logotherapy is education to responsibility not only for the patient but also for the therapist. It is the responsibility of the therapist to pull the patients out from their existential vacuum and point toward a meaningful existence. It is her responsibility to say "no" to patients who feel dependent on unfortunate determinants which hinder their personal development. A physician too has the responsibility to say "no" to a fatty diet if his patient suffers from a gall ailment. It is not sufficient to ask him: "So you like to eat fatty food?"

NAIVE QUESTION ASKING

There is, however, an exception to this rule of using the logotherapeutic dialogue as a challenge to the client. Some clients come to the therapist not primarily to seek counseling but to unburden themselves of their worries and to find validation. If the therapist does not provide this validation, or is not ready to listen quietly, the clients may become aggressive and oppose whatever the therapist suggests. Cooperation between therapist and patient then becomes even more difficult. For such cases I have developed the "naive questioning" technique. Here the clients' rebellious attitude toward all advice is used by seemingly supporting their negative and unhealthy ideas and then challenging them to rebel against their own attitudes. This method often leads to an "aha" experience and a turnabout in their point of view. With more sophisticated clients one can lay it on a little thick to make them see that unhealthy attitudes often appear ridiculous. They will get the point and move away from their own negative, now slightly exaggerated attitudes. Other more simple-minded clients, like the mother in the case below, don't even notice what the therapist is aiming at. The outcome is the same: guided by the therapist, they reject their own unhealthy viewpoint because, deep within, they know it is unhealthy. This method combines elements of paradoxical intention, grains of their innate wisdom, a bit of humor, a dose of human understanding—making it a truly logotherapeutic composition.

Case # 21:

Marie was a widow with an eight-year-old boy, Roland. This child had great difficulties in school, repeated first grade, and was about to be sent to a special school for emotionally handicapped children. Marie spent every afternoon with him, helping him with his homework, giving him extra spelling exercises although the boy developed fits of temper and tried to conceal his homework. Marie came to me bristling with arguments, mainly against the oft-heard advice to allow her son more leisure time.

Fragments of the dialogue:

Marie: I only want what is best for my Roland. Some day he'll realize that a boy must do his lessons. It's for his own good. What will happen to him if he has to go to a special school? Who'll give him a job after that? What kinds of classmates will he meet there?

Lukas: Yes, I can understand this. Your concern about Roland shows me that you are a real mother, the way a mother should be.

M: I can't just sit back and watch him fail. He has to study.

L: You are thinking of his happiness.

M: Yes, his happiness is all I want.

L: (after a pause): Tell me, how was it in your own childhood? Did schoolwork come easily?

M: Well, not really. Spelling was especially difficult, but I had to learn it anyway. All those dictation exercises . . . It still gives me the shivers to think about it.

L: Did they give you that many dictation exercises in school?

M: No, but my mother did. She was very strict, always ready with the ruler. She always said: Sit down and work! Not like the children today who spend hours in front of TV . . . that didn't even exist then.

L: So your mother was strict. Did she restrict your play time?

M: Restrict? I didn't know what free time was! My mother was an ambitious woman; she wanted me to become a nurse, or even a teacher. She had lots of plans for me. Oh well, so I became a housewife and a mother. She meant well, my mother did. She had her definite ideas, and no fooling around. Right after school it was dictation, dictation, dictation.

L: (naive therapeutic question): That must have been very pleasant for you.

M: (surprised): Pleasant? How come? No, no! What do you mean?

L: (naive): Well, I just thought, because you are doing something like this with Roland, and I know you want him to have a happy childhood.

M: You mean, I'm acting like my mother did? Yes, but he's a boy. He has to become something.

L: Tell me, what was the happiest period in your life?

M: Well . . . as I think about it, that was the time when I was newly married. I had no child yet, had moved away from my parents, my husband let me manage the household in my own way. I didn't know much but I learned from experience, and if something went wrong I tried again. That was the time, I think, when I really grew up and knew what I wanted. Yes, that was the best time of my life!

L: (naive): Then I guess Roland will have to wait a few years until he experiences the best time of his life.

M: Roland? Do you really think he feels the way I did as a child?

L: (naive): Well, I don't know. You know him better than I do. Maybe he feels different than you did. Maybe he enjoys your helping him with his homework. Maybe he doesn't care to learn from experience the way you did as a young woman.

M: No, no! That's right, the boy is exactly like me! I'm sure he hates my strictness . . . (scared) Do you think I'm like my mother?

L: (naive): Oh, that couldn't be. You want Roland to be happy but from what you said about your mother, she didn't really make you happy.

M: Yes, I want him to be happy, but I wonder how *he* feels about it. Maybe I'm making him unhappy while I'm doing what I think is best for him. I'm all mixed up now. Is it possible that Roland has been unhappy all along? That he'll be happy only after he's moved away from me? (sobbing) Oh God, oh God!

L: Lots of young women make the same mistakes their parents did. They have no example to follow except the example of their parents, and the pattern is passed on from generation to generation. If you put Roland under such pressure, with no opportunity for him to think for himself, he may do the same with his children, and this will go on and on. Someone, at some point, must break the chain. I really think you can do it. With a little help from us here and with all the love you feel for your son, you could become a first-rate mother so that Roland later will say: My happiest time was my childhood at home. My father was gone, but my mother— she was my best companion!

M: I'd like that, Frau Doktor, yes, I'd like that very much. Please help me!

After this change of attitude, the mother was open to a therapy program of encouragement and reinforcement, and we acted out the homework situation in psychodrama. Roland's ability to concentrate improved considerably and the repressed boy became a lively youngster.

The naive questioning technique differs radically from the discussion techniques of other therapies. In the above example, the question "That must have been very pleasant for you" was the starting point. Rogers' nondirective therapy would have worded the question: "Your mother really put a lot of pressure on you" (mirroring). Psychoanalysis would have gone into childhood memories (perhaps Oedipus complex). Behavior therapy would have blocked out the past, drawn a base line, agreed on a therapy goal, and suggested a step-by-step procedure, starting out with the assumption that present demands were too heavy. Although this was true in Marie's case, it would not have worked without the logotherapeutic approach which helped Marie change her attitude. Once that had occurred, a form of behavior therapy could be launched, but first her confidence in Roland's abilities, the acceptance of his weaknesses, and her trust in his future development had to be strengthened. The statement, "that must have been very pleasant for you" was an appeal to the defiant power of her human spirit to take a stand and make a decision on her own.

In psychiatric practice it often becomes evident that deep behind the problems stated by the clients lies an unhealthy attitude. Their problems can be reduced or at least made bearable if their attitude is modified to one that is positive, psychohygienically healthy, and oriented toward goals and meanings.

A modification of attitudes is especially useful for mothers whose children have grown up and become independent, whose husbands are still working, and who themselves have been busy caring for the family. They may succumb to depressions which cannot be explained simply by the menopause. Behind their depression lie the anxious questions: "What am I still good for? Who needs me? What shall I do with my life? What meaning does my life now have?"

Many women and mothers who ask themselves these questions are able to fill their lives with a meaningful content, except those who have already found a negative answer. They no longer ask: "What is my life still good for?" but declare: "My life is no longer good for anything." Such an unhealthy attitude triggers a depression whose roots are found in an existential frustration. Therapy must start by restoring their capacity to again ask the question, to give up their negative fixed answer. They must be led back to the search for meaning that had existed before they found the life content now lost. Only when they raise the old question again can they find new answers. The therapist can help them in their search.

To Case #19

The 55-year-old woman whose birthday crisis I discussed before suffered from an endogenous depression which came in a cycle of about every two years. After her children had left home she was in danger of developing a noogenic depression in interim periods. To prevent this, it was necessary to expand her horizon of interests. I began by asking her what she had been doing with her life. She talked in great detail about her work in a home with a husband and four children, especially during and after the war when her means were extremely limited. She had sewn all the clothing herself, mostly by hand, she had knitted sweaters sold in stores to stretch her limited household budget, and had made all the children's toys with her own hands. I asked her if she had not wanted to do other things, beyond the chores of everyday life. "Oh yes," she replied. "I've always wanted to do *petit-point* for wall pictures, but the material was too expensive, and they didn't have such good instructions as they have today."

I asked her about her other dreams. What had she wanted to do but had never had the time? "Well," she said, "I'd have liked to do embroidering. But the material was so tough, it was hard to work with. There were many things I had no time for—stamps, for instance. My father left me a whole boxful. I never had time to sort them . . . I've always wanted to have pen pals in foreign countries but I can't speak any foreign language. I'd have gotten letters with stamps from India, maybe Australia . . . I like to work with details, looking at stamps with a magnifying glass, embroidery, also working with wax—but life passed me by so fast . . ." "Life has *not* passed you," I reminded her. "It is just different now. You didn't have the time to do all the things you wanted to do but you can do them now, as a reward for the years of labor. Now is your chance— don't miss it. Life is giving you a gift—accept it. You never thought of yourself, you were always there for your family. Now think of yourself, even if you're not used to it. Why shouldn't you do *petit-point* for wall pictures? You have the time, and instructions and excellent materials are available. And why shouldn't you sort your stamps and perhaps swap with other collectors? There are people in many countries who want pen pals to practice their German. You can now reshape your life according to what it offers now! Things have changed. You no longer need to sew clothes from rough materials. But that doesn't mean you are useless. You can buy yourself ready-made clothes of soft and beautiful materials. And instead of telling yourself you are no longer needed to work all day in your home, you can tell yourself: "I can finally do all those things for which I never had time!"

The woman had never viewed her present life from this angle. She decided to make a small *petit-point* picture for each of her children, and also one, in memory of her dead daughter—a mountain motif her daughter had loved. She decided to keep this picture and hang it in her living room. The eagerness with which she went to work helped her over many hours of depression. By restoring her capacity to search for meaning she realized the opportunities that lay dormant in her "empty" life.

This is the fourth step of logotherapeutic intervention: the expansion of meaning possibilities. Once the identification of the clients with their symptoms is loosened by self-distancing (Step 1) and new, positive attitudes to an unchangeable situation are found (Step 2), the symptoms become at least bearable (Step 3) and new and positive factors that can fill the present life situation can be recognized (Step 4).

The therapist will do well to follow this sequence: First, modify attitudes toward symptoms, then work on attitudes toward negative factors, and finally on those toward positive factors. As long as clients are in the grip of their symptoms they will hardly be able to endure negative factors; as long as they have not attained a healthy attitude toward the negative content of their lives they will not be able to search for the positive. These steps gradually lead the clients away from their egocentricity and strengthen their capacity for self-transcendence: the symptoms are most closely linked with the ego and negative factors weigh people down more than positive factors can please them. When the clients become aware of the positive, they can forget their ego, and they become psychologically healthy.

The Viennese philosopher Leo Gabriel once said, "The animal *is* the world, the human being *has* the world." To "have" the world means not to be its victim, but to be able to take a stand toward it. This is a specifically human capacity, not found in the dimension of body and psyche which we share with other animals. It is the expression of the human spirit and must not be neglected in psychotherapy.

5

The Application of
Paradoxical Intention

Paradoxical intention is essentially a modification of attitudes centered on a symptom. Those who do not know its theoretical base are surprised at the results and suspect something like a magician's trick. But those familiar with its workings realize what a tremendous human resource has been neglected and can now be used.

The application of paradoxical intention is easy and, in almost every case, successful. What is difficult is to create the preconditions for the application which includes a prominent self-distancing. It is absolutely necessary for paradoxical intention that the clients be consciously aware that they are not identified with the feelings dominating them, but that they can choose an attitude toward those feelings and even defy them. The defiant power of the spirit must be sufficiently aroused before paradoxical intention can be applied.

Research in brain physiology has shown that the various areas of the human brain—the midbrain and the cerebrum—came into existence during two different evolutionary epochs. We now know that the human reaction to a stimulus takes place simultaneously on two levels: the level of the midbrain and the level of the cerebrum.

Let's assume the following situation: From an apartment comes the enticing fragrance of freshly baked cake. In the midbrain, the signal "cake" releases, in the presence of biological readiness (hunger), certain functions of appetite, such as increased saliva. At the same time there is a conscious reaction in the cerebrum which makes cake-eating desirable or tempting. However, if the midbrain, for whatever reason, has not reacted to the stimulus, the cerebrum does not register the corresponding emotions. The midbrain, therefore, is the first to decide whether or not the cake seems

73

tempting. Here our freedom is limited to a lower, physical level: we cannot arbitrarily decide what our emotions should be—what is agreeable or disagreeable, attractive or repulsive, desirable or undesirable. But now the cognitive superstructure comes into play. Our cerebrum not only automatically registers our emotions, it also is the place where we make decisions according to our will. However tempting the freshly baked cake may smell, and however much saliva our midbrain may produce, it is our cerebrum that makes the final decision: whether, for instance, we'll break into the apartment and steal a piece of cake. Some people may not be very hungry and not even care for cake, and will still succumb to the temptation to steal the cake; while others may be so hungry that they literally drool and still resist the temptation.

Here lies a tremendous possibility for human achievement. We can choose our emotions no more than animals can, but we can take a stand, we can control our emotions by our will. We are no longer the slaves of the midbrain as other animals are; we made the evolutionary leap into the dimension of the spirit, and thus have attained free will. It's not complete freedom. We are free from the dominating influence of our emotions in only a small area, but within that area emotions have lost their power over us.

In this marginal area of freedom the logotherapist can operate. This is the area where paradoxical intention can be applied. The patients need to be assured that here is the place where they can take a stand toward their emotions, and that's why—as a first step—they must learn to distinguish between what their (often exaggerated) emotions urge them to do, and what they want to do.

Case # 22:

One of my phobic patients would come to the session, complaining: "Today is especially bad; I hardly dared step out of the house. I couldn't get myself to take the bus, it was so crowded. I had to walk all the way to see you. I'm pooped!" And she would drop into a chair.

My reply to her was: "Did you bring your fear in here with you, or did you leave it on the street?" At first she didn't understand what I meant, and said her fear just overwhelmed her, there was nothing she could do. Then again it left, without rhyme or reason.

This may be so, I told her, but basically she was always the same person who was able to think, act, plan, and decide to come to see me, and sometimes even to take the bus despite the occasional attacks of fear which she had not learned to handle properly. In our therapy, I explained, she would learn this, and then "the fear" could try to frighten her as often as it wanted to, but it would succeed less and less. She would soon be able to chase it away. In this manner I tried to change her unhealthy obsessive attitude of "I am full of fear, I tremble with fear" to the more detached attitude of "I am a normal person, only sometimes I fight against some unfounded and unimportant feelings of anxiety."

Once clients see the separation between their health and their exaggerated feelings of fear and obsession, they can be introduced to paradoxical intention. Instead of fighting the fears and obsessions, they learn to paradoxically wish to bring about the very thing they have feared and see what happens.

What happens is—nothing. Wishing and fearing are two opposites that cancel each other out. We cannot wish it were evening and at the same time fear that evening will come.

For instance: A man who fears he will faint in an elevator has to enter the elevator with the firm wish to collapse. He will find that the more he tries to faint the less he will be able to, because only the exaggerated fear of collapsing could cause his body to actually produce something like a fainting spell. Remember: *The body is affected.* But the wish to collapse "takes the wind out of the sails of the fear" (as Frankl puts it). The patient can no longer fear, there are no automatic body reactions to the fear—no spasms, no increased blood pressure, no outbreak of perspiration, nothing. A collapse is impossible.

This seems simple, in theory at least. But the application is often not so simple. Patients who have lived in horror of something, are all of a sudden expected to wish for this very thing. Their first reaction is that this is beyond their strength, no one can ask them to do that. Obviously they need more help than the mere advice to wish for what they fear. Now the human spirit has to be activated. Not only does every crisis have its opportunity and every suffering its meaning, every fear has its adversary, namely a sense of humor. Paradoxical intention gets rid of exaggerated and unfounded fears through ridicule.

There is the story of a medieval robber knight who frightened everyone in the country. His reputation was such that no one even tried to fight him. One day he fell from his horse so clumsily that part of his armor got caught in the saddle. To prevent his horse from dragging him, he grabbed the horse's tail and stumbled behind it. This looked so funny that all who saw it laughed; and from that day on the power of the robber knight was broken. The more people laughed about him the more their fear disappeared, and the more their fear disappeared the more they resisted him until he was conquered.

This is the principle of paradoxical intention. It helps the patients laugh at their fears and obsessions. When this succeeds confidence in their own stability and security returns and the nightmare of neurosis is conquered.

Case # 23:

Once I practiced elevator riding with a client in the 20-floor city hall in Kaiserslautern. The woman had a horror of elevators, spiral staircases, funiculars, and long echoing corridors. She was afraid she would get sick and dizzy, would be unable to breathe, and would faint.

Before we entered the elevator I asked her to faint many times on the way up, possibly once between every floor for a total of twenty. I promised to wake her up quickly so she wouldn't miss fainting on the next floor. "As long as we go up 20 floors we want to experience 20 fainting spells," I said, paradoxically intending, "let's make it a clean sweep!"

The humorous formulations immediately defused her initial fear which made it possible for her to try the therapeutic experiment. After we passed the first floor I pretended to be disappointed that she was still erect. On the second floor I shook my head impatiently and urged her to hurry up if she wanted to fill her quota of faints. On the fifth floor I told her angrily that she had promised at least one collapse and it was high time to keep her word, and from the tenth floor on I implored her to use all her efforts to at least break out in perspiration.

After my client arrived laughing and unfainted at the top floor we celebrated her victory over her fear in the roof cafeteria with a glass of lemonade, and then went to work practicing elevator riding with paradoxical intention. Before the day was over she succeeded, without my help, to ride up and down city hall without harmful consequences.

The formulations the patient learns to use must be humorous enough to eliminate serious misgivings and to defuse the fear. At first, the patient practices these formulations with the therapist; later, alone and facing the feared situation. Fun, mockery, and exaggeration can be used to wrap the fear in ridicule. What makes us smile cannot cause horror. But the patients must never get the impression that the therapist laughs about *them;* they must see that they themselves, with the help of the therapist, laugh about their own ridiculous fears and emotional absurdities. That's why the self-distancing between client and symptom is so important. As long as the clients see themselves as identical with their fears, how can one ridicule the other?

The first few times that patients practice their formulations they tend to be skeptical, hesitant. They don't know whether to laugh or weep. They do not really believe in success and feel insecure. Many patients expected therapy of a different sort. They thought the therapist would explore their past, interpret their dreams, analyze their childhood rather than question their fears in a humorous manner. That's why the initial phase is highly critical, and the therapist must make every effort to consider the individuality of each patient. Experience will teach the logotherapist how to find the right dose of formulations for the patient. The basic trust, the human bridge between patient and therapist, must not be shaken because this is the path on which confidence in success will eventually pass from therapist to patient so that patients will get to the point where they will really wish for what they fear. From then on the therapeutic process continues almost by itself.

To Case # 22:

I remember how the young woman who feared crowded streets and buses (and whom I kept asking whether she had brought the fear into my office), one day began to respond to my efforts and said, "Yes, today I left my fear outside. I can come to you without fear. I know you will help me."

This was the opening for me. I said, "Good. Let's put on our coats and go look for your fear. If you left it outside we can find it. It's not fair to your fear to simply lose it after you have been friends for such a long time." In this manner I tried to prepare her for paradoxical intention—no more frantic fights against the fear, no desperate flights from the fear, but a humorous searching for it.

My patient was reluctant to go out on the street with me, but once we were there things happened as expected. The more I asked her to finally get me to the place where she had left the fear and where she had last seen it, the less she was able to feel afraid. Eventually we took the bus to her home and she burst into tears, saying that she had never felt so free of anxiety strolling through the city. But she still gave my presence credit for her success, and it required several sessions of practice for her to find the courage to go into a crowded street by herself, "searching for her lost fear." When she saw that the method worked when she was by herself, the healing process started in earnest, and today she no longer needs to look for her fear because, as she says, "it can no longer be found."

Paradoxical intention is especially indicated for phobias and obsessive compulsions, also for hysteroid and psychosomatic difficulties and for unwanted behavior patterns that are triggered by certain situations. Enough is known today to justify a treatment of the symptoms as is done by desensitization in behavior therapy or by paradoxical intention in logotherapy. The vicious cycle of fear only rarely has "deeper causes" but develops more or less by chance.

To understand the effects of paradoxical intention we must start with the phenomenon of "anticipatory anxiety" and observe the cycle mechanism it triggers. In practice, this is what happens: Something disagreeable happens in a certain situation. It upsets us and we develop an anticipatory anxiety that it may happen again when we face a similar situation. The anxiety causes us to think about it excessively, makes us insecure and expectant of repetition. This is exactly what makes recurrence more likely. It is a law of nature that fear brings about what is feared. The more we fearfully expect the return of a disagreeable happening, the more likely it is to recur in a similar situation. If it happens again our fear is confirmed and we are certain the pattern will be repeated. Fear causes anticipatory anxiety, and anticipatory anxiety causes fear—a vicious cycle is formed from which there seems no escape, at least not without help from a therapist.

That anticipatory anxiety can actually bring about the disagreeable happening was shown in an independent hospital study. The entire staff was given a blood test to investigate their resistance to various diseases. A few weeks later the rumor was purposely spread that a severe typhus infection had occurred in the hospital, and the entire staff was quarantined. Again a blood test was given and each person was asked in a questionnaire about his or her level of anxiety in general and about the infection specifically.

It was found that those persons who indicated a high level of anxiety were also those who had a reduced level of anti-toxins. This meant that in case of a real typhus epidemic they would have less resistance to the "feared happening" than their less anxiety-ridden colleagues. On a purely physical level fear had made the occurrence of the feared event more likely. This may also explain why doctors and nurses who work with infectious diseases do not get sick themselves: They do not fear the sickness and retain maximum resistance.

All this does not mean that fear is always a negative factor. Too little fear may also have dangerous consequences. Mountain climbers consider two types of people in danger: The careless ones who go ahead with insufficient equipment and information about expected conditions, and those who are afraid of falling. While carelessness can be corrected by experience and learning, fears are difficult to overcome because phobics see themselves trapped in the vicious cycle of fear and anticipatory anxiety.

Suppose a teen-age apprentice is called to the office of his boss. Because of the excitement, or even because the room is warm, he perspires and the boss makes a harmless remark about it. The next time the apprentice is called to the boss the boy becomes afraid he may perspire again. He carefully wipes his face, enters the office, and the fear of perspiring drives the sweat from his pores. After the second experience he is certain that the third time he faces the boss he will be dripping with sweat. His anticipatory anxiety increases and is confirmed every time. He tries to run away from it, avoids the boss's office, calls in sick when he expects to be summoned, takes tranquilizers, and gets caught more and more in a desperate cycle. His anxiety spreads to other situations. He fears he may sweat when talking to any grown-up; he withdraws, becomes a loner, his shyness increases, and he finds less courage to face people. He sees a doctor who prescribes new tranquilizers. The boss cannot use an apprentice who gets sick so often and fires him. This failure throws the young man even more into the grip of fear. He develops a general fear of life, his self-confidence diminishes, his body is affected and produces, in addition to perspiration, palpitations of the heart and sleep disturbances, and one day the young man is "finished."

Therapy can break this vicious cycle either at the point of the anticipatory anxiety or at the point of sweating. The therapeutic treatment of sweating, a physical symptom, must use physical means such as relaxation training or medication. The therapeutic treatment of anticipatory anxiety, a psychological disturbance, must use psychological means such as paradoxical intention. Frankl speaks of a "pincer movement"—attacking the problem from both the physical and the psychological angle. But beyond that, the treatment must include strengthening the dimension of the spirit. Self-distancing from the symptoms activates forces that help the patient defy the vicious cycle and build self-confidence. Because paradoxical intention reduces the anticipatory anxiety, the symptom fades. If the symptom is at least reduced, the anticipatory anxiety is lowered.

In our example, the apprentice was encouraged to intend, using humorous formulations, exactly what he feared, namely sweating. He learned to tell himself that he "would show his boss just how much he could "sweat." He would perspire a puddle in the room so the boss could swim away in it. That would be a good way to get rid of the boss, as well as his fear of the boss.

The formulations sound exaggerated because they *have* to sound exaggerated enough so they won't work as autosuggestions. Only when the formulations are ridiculous enough is it possible for the patient not to take them seriously. The purpose of this technique is to bring patients to the point where they will not take the formulations and their whole unfounded fear seriously.

The formulations function as a go-between: The patients' attitude toward the formulations is transferred to their attitude toward their emotional disorder. The more exaggerated and ridiculous the formulations, the more exaggerated and ridiculous the phobias (and obsessive compulsions) seem. The neurotic cycle is broken, the fear is deprived of its power, the consequences of the fear are reduced and new phobic attacks become less likely. The vicious cycle is reversed in the direction of the patient's health.

The third logotherapeutic step, the reduction of symptoms, is achieved gradually. In our example, the apprentice realizes that he is unable to perspire even when he tries hard, the fear loses its terror, he begins to laugh about it, the specter disappears.

With paradoxical intention there are almost no relapses because the patients have learned its application and can make up their own appropriate formulations when new fears threaten.

Skeptics have argued that the danger with paradoxical intention is not so much a relapse, but a possible spreading of the symptoms. Because the deep-seated causes of the existing symptom are not sufficiently unearthed, so they reason, other symptoms will make their appearance. Their hypothesis, however, is too simple. Regardless of whether or not a deep-seated cause is present, the existing symptom itself becomes the cause of a chain of new symptoms. Phobias and obsessions, however they are caused, bring about a lower self-image, a pattern of avoidance, a withdrawal from activities, and often the conviction of being a complete failure, and even suicide.

Therapists cannot afford to disregard the present symptoms and search for imaginary causes while valuable time slips by and a new chain of symptoms is formed. The deeper causes can always be explored later if necessary, but first the chain of unhappy consequences must be interrupted; the symptoms must be reduced. When this is accomplished, positive feedback reactions bring new confidence and help patients overcome and cope with any deeper causes that may exist.

OBSESSIVE COMPULSIONS

What has been said so far has referred principally to phobias. But paradoxical intention is also applicable to obsessive compulsions.

While people understand phobics to some extent, they tend to reject obsessive compulsive patients as "crazy." Everyone experiences fears but compulsions seem incomprehensible. People cannot understand or sympathize with persons who imagine they have to push others in front of a bus, set fire, wash their hands continuously, or check again and again the door they have just locked.

Even more important is to free obsessive compulsives from their vicious cycle and lead them toward a healthy self-understanding. Their vicious cycle, however, is different from that of phobics. Phobics actually experience what they fear (they panic, blush, perspire, stutter) but obsessive neurotics never experience the feared event. They do not push people in front of buses, set fires, or get sick more than those who wash their hands less often, and they always lock their doors carefully. Still they suffer from their fears because they do not see that their fears are groundless. They have developed behavior patterns that prevent them from ever experiencing the feared situation which would help them see that the feared event would not take place even if they dropped their compulsive behavior.

Those who never go near a bus stop because they fear they will push people in front of a bus never learn that they would not do it if they stood at the stop. Those who wash their hands for hours never know that they would be just as healthy without that precaution. They are never certain whether their avoidance behavior is sufficient to prevent the feared event, and this uncertainty reinforces their fear and keeps the vicious cycle going.

In the case of phobias, paradoxical intention intervenes at the point of anticipatory anxiety, and indirectly prevents the fear from occurring. In the case of obsessive compulsion, it intervenes at the point of fear and indirectly eliminates the uncertainty. For the phobics, paradoxical intention makes the fear of "something" disappear; for obsessive compulsives it makes the patients experience that this "something" does not happen, and thus eliminates the tortuous uncertainty.

"Push me in front of the bus!" the psychotherapist tells the patient, standing next to him at the bus stop. This sounds very risky but isn't, because the obsessive compulsive is completely harmless. He never does what he fears; only he never knows it.

"Set fire to everything!" the psychotherapist tells the patients, handing them a box of matches. They must be exposed to the anxiety provoking situation so they can see that they will not do what they fear. Patients must experience that they can hold matches without setting fire, stand at a bus stop without pushing people in front of the bus. This, for them, is a liberating "aha" experience; they see that they act normal, even if they face a situation that tempts them to do what they have always feared. (Of course, this method is counterindicated for people who are hostile and really want to kill people, or who really are arsonists. A diagnosis must establish that they are obsessive compulsives who do not really want to do a certain thing but are merely afraid that they might).

Obsessive compulsives who have always believed they have not locked their apartment door securely enough, are told to let the door stand wide open so the thieves in the neighborhood can help themselves. Too many things have accumulated anyway. Patients with a handwashing compulsion invite all the germs in the neighborhood to a giant party on their hands. They do not want to exclude a single germ.

Paradoxical intention can achieve success fast, as soon as the patients realize: "Now look at that! I'm not doing it!" or "What do you know; it doesn't happen!"

Some patients are well-suited for paradoxical intention. They have a sense of humor, can achieve self-distancing, understand how the method works, and cooperate when they have their "aha" experience. Other patients do not have the predisposition for paradoxical intention and make it difficult for the therapist. There are the "yes-but" types, people who always find something wrong, or who feel ridiculed or offended when the therapist offers paradoxical formulations. Some have a definite expectation of what the therapy "should" be like and resent the unorthodox method.

In such cases it is important for the therapist to demonstrate her identification with the patients, speak the formulations with them, go out with them to participate in their practice of paradoxical intention. This not only sets an example, it also shows them that she takes their problems seriously even though the formulations are ridiculous. If the emphasis of therapy is on the "we" the logotherapist is likely to be accepted even if the client had different expectations.

Case #24:

One of my patients had a mirror compulsion that prompted her to run to a mirror up to 20 times a day to make sure that her hair was sufficiently well-groomed. She resisted paradoxical intention until I offered to participate with her in a game of "hair rumpling": We would see who could rumple our hair more thoroughly by attacking it with all ten fingers. Afterwards we ran hand in hand around the block, all the while paradoxically intending to show all passers-by just how wildly our hair "stood on end." When someone passed us without paying any attention, we roughed up our hair a bit more because it obviously was not disheveled enough. This game won the cooperation of the patient who up to then had resisted all paradoxical formulations. Of course, no one paid any attention to us. Who nowadays cares whether someone's hair is well-groomed? My patient realized this and was able to overcome her compulsion to go to the mirror by paradoxically wishing, "Let my hair stand on end. Let it be a mess!" After eight weeks her mirror compulsion was gone.

Also difficult are patients who remain apathetic or skeptical, maintaining that it is the therapist's job to treat them and it is not up to them to contribute to their own cure. They dutifully repeat the formulations that are suggested, without any inner commitment. The problem is to get them to really mean what they merely parrot. Such patients easily slip from the paradoxical attitude into autosuggestion, and that can be dangerous.

Case #25:

This patient came to me for marriage counseling. He suffered from a compulsive car phobia. Whenever he drove on a road lined with trees or telegraph poles he was overcome by the thought that he would steer the car directly into a tree. "Trees magnetize me," he said unhappily. He had developed an avoidance pattern: he stopped the car, parked it on the side of the road, stopped another car, told the driver his car had broken down and asked for a ride to the next telephone. His wife had to pick up the car, which led to repeated quarrels.

The man was an extremely difficult patient. He refused to accept my assurance that he would not drive into a tree—only careless people would do that, and he was super careful. When I offered him humorous formulations which he was to say to himself while driving, he was convinced that wishing for an accident would immediately bring it about.

Here again the application of paradoxical intention required my personal participation. I sat next to him in the car and asked him to drive around. "We'll select some good trees to bump into," I told him. "Show me some into which you'd enjoy crashing." "I can show you a road which fills me with horror," he said and drove to a narrow country road lined on both sides with beautiful old trees. When he stopped at its beginning I challenged him: "OK, now drive on this gorgeous road in a zigzag. We want to bump into all those trees, alternating once on the right, then on the left, then the right again. Go ahead and crash. Don't miss a single tree. We want to get to know them all." I kept talking this way until the man, soaked in sweat but driving in a straight line, arrived at the end of the road. "You were right; nothing happened," he said, amazed. "I'll try it again."

I welcomed this idea but asked him, this time, to say the paradoxical formulations himself. And here I learned how paradoxical intention can turn into autosuggestion. The patient began: "I want to drive in a zigzag, bumping into the tree on the right, then on the left . . . always zigzag . . . I'm going to crash into a tree on . . . the right . . . right away I'm going to crash . . ."

The "I want to" had become an anxious "I'm going to." The proud smile about the fear had given way to a trembling anxiety, the self-distancing was shattered, and he was back in the grip of his compulsion. This was an emergency. I quickly had to restore the ridiculousness to the formulations and get rid of the autosuggestion. "Well," I said, "we have now bumped into half the trees. Crashing in zigzag is a lot of fun, but now let's bump into the trees while driving in reverse." The smile reappeared, he picked up my suggestion, invented his own paradoxical formulations for driving forward and backward. Of course, he didn't even come near a tree. We practiced this therapeutic driving until the patient was able to do it without my presence. From then on he made good progress in his recovery.

If a patient really does not have the strength to wish for the feared event, the neurosis can be taken into a therapeutic pincer movement. This means that the fear, as well as its physical consequences, must be reduced at the same time and by different means. Autogenic training and medication are possible supplements of paradoxical intention.

Case #26:

The patient was a physically strong man who liked jogging in the woods until one day, probably from overexertion, he suddenly collapsed. From that moment on he became uncertain about his physical fitness and was afraid his knees would suddenly give in and he would collapse again. As a consequence he actually felt his knees go soft and had to sit down. After this had happened twice and he had the embarrassing experience of having to sit on the curb of the sidewalk, he hardly dared leave home and insisted on walking only on trails with plenty of benches.

Here was a classic case of an anxiety cycle mechanism: An incidental negative event had triggered an anxiety which caused physical problems, mostly vascular and muscular spasms. The patient had such a terror that "his knees would give in" that he was unable to use paradoxical formulations ("there's nothing more pleasant than having soft knees") whenever there was the least sign of an approaching attack. He immediately fled in panic to the nearest place to sit.

After failing with paradoxical intention, I decided to use the therapeutic pincer on his neurosis. We practiced autogenic training in all its seven phases until we were able to follow his inner command to relax in any situation, and to calm his inner agitation. Then we agreed on the following procedure: He would take short walks in the woods and use paradoxical formulations *before* he felt any anticipatory anxiety. If the anxiety still overcame him (and with it the weakness in his knees) he was to reduce the spasms with autogenic training. After feeling relaxed again he was to switch to paradoxical formulations to prevent a recurrence of the anticipatory anxiety. Using this alternating rhythm, he was to take his walks in the woods where he would not be seen by many people. He was to note the longest time span he was able to walk without difficulties.

The patient tried this several times and noted the time spans: ¼ hour, ¾ hours, 2½ hours, 1 hour, 2½ hours, 4 hours, an entire afternoon.

Happily he reported that during his last walk in the woods he started with the paradoxical formulations, looking forward to using autogenic training when the anticipatory anxiety came—but it never came. Without realizing it he had focused the paradoxical intention not only on the symptoms (' "I wish my knees would finally give in") but also on the expectation ("When will that anticipatory anxiety finally get to me?"). It became impossible for his knees to give in; his body remained stable. Using the same system, he extended his walks to city areas and populated streets which allowed him, at the slightest hint of discomfort, to lean against a wall and restore his "inner peace" with autogenic formulations, before continuing his walk. After a while he no longer needed the calming down; the paradoxical formulations were sufficient to prevent anticipatory anxiety, and after half a year he did not even need this last crutch. The cycle mechanism of fear was broken.

This example illustrates how well logotherapeutic methods can be combined and the importance of the personal participation of the therapist and the willingness to improvise. Even the best technique cannot replace personal involvement.

ENDOGENOUS DEPRESSIONS

Frankl has warned not to use paradoxical intention for endogenous depressions. These are physically caused depressions that come and go without apparent reason. During periods of depression patients are not likely to appreciate the humorous formulations. They would consider them a mockery of their condition. To say to an endogenously depressed person during the depth of a depression, "Come on, try crying a little harder," is more than such a patient can be expected to bear. There also is the danger that endogenously depressed patients may take the formulations seriously and transform them into dangerous autosuggestions.

Although endogenously depressed persons cannot be advised to "wish" for sadness, as paradoxical intention would do, they can be advised not to fight their depression. Such patients need not "pull themselves together," as they often desperately try to do, they only need to patiently bear their depressive phase. Even this attitude of composure will help relieve their suffering. Frankl has shown repeatedly that it is justified for the physician to assure endogenously depressed patients that they have done nothing to become sick (thus, they are "guiltless") and that they need do nothing to get well again; if they don't believe that, it only confirms the diagnosis that they are really suffering from an endogenous depression which is characterized by symptoms of doubt and pessimism. And it also confirms the favorable prognosis that is justified for such depressions. Such arguments by the physician greatly help the patients objectify their sickness and gain distance from it.

Self-distancing offers the best chance for endogenously depressed patients, supplementing their treatment through medication. They are helped to see their mood of sadness as an unavoidable but temporary condition and to be confident that the sadness will pass and they will again see meaning and joy in life. If the therapist succeeds in keeping alive hope in the patients, even during the periods of darkest helplessness, the crisis is contained. Fate has no power over those who have found a positive attitude toward it.

The fact that patients can master their problems by seeing an opportunity behind a crisis, discovering a meaning behind unavoidable suffering, smiling about their phobias and obsessions, and accepting their depression as an act of fate is proof alone of the existence of a human dimension that transcends their physiopsychological functions. If this were not so our patients would be helplessly trapped in their crises, sufferings, anxieties, and depressions. But they are not trapped. Their specifically human qualities enable them to distance themselves from their difficulties, and even transcend them.

It is said that we psychotherapists can look down into the abyss of the human psyche. But we can also look up, in amazement and awe, to the achievements of the human spirit.

6

The Application of Dereflection

Self-examination leads to healthy self-assessment. Exaggerated self-observation, however, may be harmful and even lead to sickness. Classical examples are insomnia and sexual dysfunctions. The more we observe our process of falling asleep and the more we focus on our expected sexual performance, the more likely that we will block these autonomic body functions. Excessive self-observation causes anxiety and "the body is affected."

When what we fear actually happens, our anxiety is heightened the next time we approach the feared situation, and the vicious cycle sets in. This is true for all body functions that should remain autonomic, such as talking, walking, or dancing. Normally, when we talk we think of *what* we say, not how the sounds are produced by our lips and tongue. If we anxiously observe ourselves to see whether we'll stutter, the likelihood of stuttering increases. Similarly, if we anxiously observe our steps when walking or dancing we are more likely to stumble. The same cause-and-effect reaction is true for other autonomic body functions such as swallowing or heartbeat. Excessive observation brings about disturbances which activate a feedback reaction and may result in psychosomatic illness.

Difficulties worsen if individual excesses are reinforced by social pressure. An illustration is today's widespread emphasis on sexual performance which, through excessive self-observation and its feedback reaction, has led to increased impotence and frigidity.

Because these disturbances concern organic functions, a diagnosis must be made to see if the problem is physiological. If it isn't, psychotherapy is indicated. Logotherapy has done considerable work to counter the unhealthy "hyperreflection" (Frankl's term).

To counteract hyperreflection, the therapy must reduce the self-observation so that autonomic body functions can be resumed undisturbed. This, however, is not easy because one cannot advise clients *not* to think of their sleep or potency. By telling them not to think about a certain subject we draw attention to that very subject. It is equally difficult not to think of anything at all. The only thing we can suggest is that they think of something *else:* The logotherapeutic method of dereflection detaches the clients from their symptoms and directs their attention to another, more positive subject.

In addition to correcting the clients' reflection, it is often necessary to dereflect their intention, because reflection and intention go hand in hand. Clients who suffer from insomnia not only think too much about falling asleep, they *want* to fall asleep. Sexual neurotics not only worry about their sexual performance, they *want* to prove their sexual prowess. This "hyperintention" (another term coined by Frankl) may also bring about psychological disturbances. Both hyperreflection and hyperintention result when people do not make use of their capacity for self-transcendence, the capacity to reach out to others. The autonomic body functions must not be directly intended by us, they must remain the automatic by-products of goals that lie outside ourselves.

A man who drops into bed at night thinking about what he has accomplished that day will soon fall asleep. A woman who in the union with her partner thinks of his pleasure instead of her own, will find sexual gratification. When patients concentrate not on themselves but on their work or their partner, the body functions automatically.

Thus, it is not only the reflection, but the intention that must also be corrected, and this may require a modification of attitudes. Patients must be guided to see the disturbed body functions as unimportant, the meaningful goals (other persons, causes, activities, experiences) as important. Only then will they focus their attention on the goals and away from their body functions, and thus find the healing self-transcendence.

To some extent, dereflection resembles autogenic training where deep relaxation is achieved not merely by autosuggestion but also by the fact that the rhythmically repeated formulations shift clients from brooding about their problems. Because the formulations have a suggestive force, they must be directed toward positive goals.

Case # 27:

Dereflection can be applied in a wide variety of situations. I once used it to help a high school student overcome his severe anxieties in school. Anton was highly intelligent and should have easily passed his tests. But when it came to examinations he concentrated on the fear that he might have forgotten all he knew, and indeed he did poorly.

He also developed typical psychosomatic stomach disorders often found in nervous students. Actually, the problem was not really a disturbed body function which should have operated automatically, unless one considers the ready recalling of learned material a body function. Nevertheless, I decided to try dereflection and suggested the following plan to his parents: For three months the topic "school" was to be avoided; instead, Anton's free-time program was to be enriched. He was to be allowed to join a soccer team requiring two practice sessions a week, and games on weekends. He also was permitted to join a choir as he had a good tenor voice and liked to sing. His electric train, which was set up in the small apartment only during holidays, was made to operate during the school season. He was encouraged to take books out of a library and to read what he wanted. For weekends, outings and picnics were planned.

The parents were skeptical. They were afraid that, with so many outside activities, Anton's average would drop even lower in class. I, too, asked myself if dereflection would work in this kind of a situation.

His parents cooperated beautifully. Whenever Anton began talking about school, they asked him about last night's choir practice, about his soccer games, or about picnic plans. After a few weeks the changes in the boy were apparent. He was lively, interested, and the more he became involved in his extra-curricular activities the more he forgot about his anxieties. I was certain of success when his mother told me after nine weeks that Anton had come home from school and during mealtime suddenly said, "Today we had a math test; I should have had a bellyache—but I didn't think of it."

After half a year, Anton's grade had improved from a C average to an *A* minus. This case confirmed my suspicion that the possibilities of dereflection were by no means exhausted by the kinds of cases generally described in the logotherapeutic literature, and that there was still room for much experimentation, improvisation and exploration.

When I began to explore the possibilities, I ran into a roadblock. Dereflection, although a specifically logotherapeutic technique, clashed with a basic logotherapeutic principle; namely, the honest, personal relationship between counselor and client. Clients are not to be manipulated. They are to be fully informed of the processes in progress so they can become partners in the common search for meaning and health. It remains the clients' responsibility to take charge of their lives and use the armory of logotherapy to achieve their goals.

When applying dereflection, however, it is not possible to keep the clients fully informed about what the counselor intends to accomplish. When clients are told not to think about their problems but rather of something else, the dereflective purpose is lost because the instruction not to think about their problem draws attention to the very thought from which they are supposed to dereflect. This dilemma can be resolved by methods that come close to "trickery." In the classical case of sexual dysfunction, for instance, an impotent man may be told that his partner must not have sex while taking some medication, but he is allowed to be with her in intimate situations. At the same time, his partner is told to let nature take its course when she sees he is ready. No longer beset by expectations from his partner, himself, or the situation, he is dereflected and the normal functions of his body again become unblocked.*

THE ALTERNATIVE LIST

To reduce "trickery" to a minimum I use dereflection by alternative lists. And I expand the application of dereflection beyond the classical cases of insomnia and sexual dysfunctioning to a variety of cases including depression and fear of failure.

---

* The treatment of sexual dysfunction by dereflection was first discussed by Frankl in 1947 (*Psychotherapie in der Praxis*, Verlag Deutike, Vienna). It precedes the methods by Masters and Johnson in the seventies.

First, I explain to my clients the connection between their symptoms and their brooding about them. We agree to work together on a scheme to reduce their hyperreflection. This assures me of their cooperation.

Next, I suggest they think of desirable, positive, and healthy activities that would enrich their lives. They are to make a list of such activities. I am available for suggestions and help with the list. The clients are also asked to write down the circumstances in which their problem seems acute and when they could try alternative activities.

Third, they are told to select one of these activities every time they are likely to hyperreflect. Only during this phase do the purposes of counselor and client diverge. The clients are told to try out their chosen activities, supposedly to determine their later use in therapy. In reality, this "preparation" for therapy is already therapy (dereflection).

The clients require some time to test their alternatives. This is valuable healing time during which attention to the problem is replaced by attention given to the testing of alternatives. The symptom is "neglected," although the clients hardly notice that the trouble subsides.

When the clients finally decide which of the alternative activities could be used for dereflection, dereflection has already taken place. They have proved to themselves that they are not the helpless victims of their depressions, fears, or whatever other problems had occupied their minds. They have broken the pattern that seemed unbreakable and gained distance from their symptoms. They have changed their self-image from "I am a depressed person," "I am a failure," or "I am impotent," to "I am a human being who has experienced depressions, failures, or impotence." They see their problems as no longer intrinsic parts of their person but rather as experiences they have acquired and from which they can free themselves.

The results, including the new self-image, may have to be fortified. Some clients have to be encouraged to continue with an alternative activity, and this may lead to new and fulfilling interests. Others will decide that they no longer need the detour of the alternate activities which they consider "childish." A Socratic dialogue will help them find their own short-range and long-range goals.

Case # 28:

The following case illustrates the application of dereflection through alternative listmaking. Martin S, 41, had been depressed and apathetic since his wife left him and their 15-year-old son Tom. Although the marriage left much to be desired, Mr. S was full of guilt and self-doubt, brooding over such questions as: Why did his wife leave him? What had he done to drive her away? and What could he have done to prevent the break-up? During the day, at work, he functioned normally ("We are very busy at the shop") but at home he sat for hours, staring holes into the air. Occasionally he was overcome by weeping he could not stop. Tom, meanwhile, had run away from home several times and had been brought back by the police. The youth authorities decided to have him sent to a boys' home, and wanted a psychological appraisal which, they said, was a matter of routine because the case was "clear-cut."

An extensive interview with Tom disclosed that he had run away because his father was inaccessible to him, and he felt lonely and unhappy. Still, he loved his father and refused to go to an institution. I then asked to see his father.

Fragments from Our Talks (Abbreviated)

I: (Dr. Lukas) Mr. S, Tom tells me you still feel bad about your wife's leaving you.

S: That's right.

I: It's been half a year. Do you think you can overcome your sorrow?

S: I don't think so. It's getting worse. And now they'll take away my boy (he weeps).

I: (after a pause) Mr. S, in my work I see a lot of people in pain. Some are facing severe grief and still are able to function. Others break down at the smallest problem.

S: Not everyone has the same strength . . .

I: True. That's why I would like to propose a plan. If you don't feel strong enough to face your pain, maybe I can help.

S: No one can help me. How do you want to help me?

I: I cannot undo what happened. But I'm trained to help, and would like to help you, too. I offer you all my knowledge and my caring in support of your own strength. I don't know if we both will be strong enough to defy your depression, but we can try.

S: I know you mean well, but I have no hope. I often told myself to pull myself together, but I can't do it. I just can't do it!

I: We can do it, together. Think about it and tell me tomorrow if you want to try.

Next day:

I: Well, Mr. S, how do you feel today?

S: I came . . . I'd like . . . to try. (Embarrassed) Tom said to me: "You know, dad, the woman, she'll help us."

I: I'm really glad. Tell me, what would you say is the worst thing about what happened with your wife?

S: What do you mean?

I: Well, what would you say weighs you down: that your wife left you, and the anger and disappointment this caused you; or the consequences of your wife's leaving—the lonely evenings, the loss of companionship, the undivided responsibility for your child?

S: You know, our marriage was not all that good. My wife was so different from me, we never were really a good match. . . (he tells about his marriage). No, it's more the consequences, the evenings alone, I always keep thinking why it happened. I just can't shake it off.

I: Tell me more about that. How does it start?

S: I don't know how. Suddenly it hits me that she is gone, that she'll never come back, whether I could have prevented it—my thoughts circle around these questions like moths around a flame. I cannot do anything against it.

I: And these thoughts prevent you from doing anything?

S: Exactly. I think that nothing makes sense, whatever I do . . .

I: And as long as you do nothing but think these thoughts, you feel paralyzed?

S: That's right. The brooding seems to fill every corner of my self. I have to make a great effort to do even the routine things that are necessary to go to bed. Only my sleep rescues me.

I: Then you would say that you could bear the end of your marriage if you were not overcome by these unhappy thoughts that choke off your strength to go on with your life?

S: Yes, I believe that's true. I didn't see it so clearly but you might be right. If I didn't have to think about it, day after day, I might be able to overcome it. But the thoughts cannot be controlled, they come by themselves.

I: During the day, when you are at work, they don't come?

S: Strange, then they don't come. We are very busy now, before Christmas, at the shop.

I: And there you feel better about yourself than at home?

S: Yes, that's true. Do you think I should work overtime?

I: Perhaps there are other things than work that can divert you from your brooding. Can you think of something? A hobby? Music? Sports? Games?

S: All these things mean nothing to me now.

I: Did you have other interests before your wife left you?

S: Well, when I think of it (he hesitates) there was always something to do. I cannot pinpoint it, some job in the house, nothing special . . .

I: You didn't have the time to go after your own interests?

S: Yes, of course, that's the way it was.

I: But now you have more time. The time you spend brooding is really free time, isn't it? You could use it to go after your interests.

S: I can't.

I: You could do many things in this time, also things together with Tom, if you were not blocked by your unhappy thoughts. We would have to find something that is stronger than your thoughts, something that interests you, that you enjoy and that diverts you from thinking about the past, something that opens new possibilities for the future. Something strong enough so you can use it as a weapon against that destructive brooding of yours. (Here I attempt to help Mr. S gain distance between himself and his symptoms.)

S: A weapon, that sounds as if . . . Isn't it a weapon against myself? I am the one who is doing the thinking, and I cannot forget, not even if I do something else.

I: No, it's not a weapon against yourself. It's a weapon against your suffering. But suffering need not produce more suffering. First, your wife left you; that brought on your lonely evenings, and now they want to take Tom away from you. But you don't have to give in. You can use your suffering as a challenge to become stronger so you can overcome it.

S: The way you say this—I really wish I could do that.

I: You only need a little patience and a little trust. Try to imagine all the things you could do to spend your evenings in a meaningful way. What could you do?

S: Well, I can imagine things, but I can enjoy nothing.

I: That doesn't matter. For the time being we'll just make a list of your personal interests, activities, hobbies, or experiences that you could try. Let's both work on this list, and then you can test which one of them you might use as a "weapon" against your compulsive and unhappy thoughts.

S: We won't find anything.

I: Perhaps you expect too much. A meaningful activity for the evening does not mean that you have to forget your wife. On the contrary. You probably have some good memories about your marriage, and those you should keep alive. You don't have to erase the past, but you can live with and in spite of your memories. What, then, would you list first for an activity?

S: (after a long pause) What I once would have liked to do . . . well, to set up a technically perfect electric train—that sounds childish, doesn't it?

I: Not at all. That's an interesting project. Do you have the parts?

S: Yes, much of it is in boxes in our attic. We probably would have to buy a few more items. Somehow there was never time for it . . .

During the next three sessions we put together a list of fifteen possible activities for the evenings and weekends. Despite his initial apathy and doubt he began to see a certain amount of fun in our "game," but he repeatedly insisted that he couldn't imagine that this could in any way help him overcome his problems. After finishing the list Mr. S receive the following instructions:

I: You thought up a nice list of interests and here it is all written down. I am adding a rating scale next to each item. Like this:

Set up electric train	$-2 -1 \ 0 +1 +2$
Go to sauna	$-2 -1 \ 0 +1 +2$
Help Tom with homework	$-2 -1 \ 0 +1 +2$
Listen to the hit parade on radio/ TV and make tape recordings	$-2 -1 \ 0 +1 +2$
Prepare salads and mayonnaise	$-2 -1 \ 0 +1 +2$
Take apart and repair old kitchen stove	$-2 -1 \ 0 +1 +2$
Grow cacti from seeds	$-2 -1 \ 0 +1 +2$
(And so on)	

Now I need your cooperation for the next 15 days. Every night when you come home from work, select one activity listed here and work on it continuously until you go to bed, without interruption, even if you think it's useless and won't bring you any relief. Keep it up, only for 15 days. On Saturdays and Sundays select something that takes more time, the train or the stove. Before you go to bed, mark how you feel on our scale. Plus 2 when you feel very satisfied, 0 when you feel so so, and −2 when you feel bad. After 15 days we'll have a good idea about which activities work well for you and can be used later in our therapy. Will you do this?

S: I guess I can do it for 15 days if you think that's important. But I can tell you right now, I'll mark nothing but minus twos.

I: That's all right. Be honest and mark just how you feel. The important thing is to keep it up. If you have difficulties, call me, I'll always be ready for you.

(Six days later I received a phone call from Mr. S)

S: I just wanted to tell you, last night when I went to bed I felt good for the first time in a long time. Tom and I had worked on the train, and close to midnight we were so tired we could hardly keep our eyes open. But you can't imagine how happy Tom was. And I had hardly thought of my troubles. Only when I brushed my teeth I realized that it's only a game and that I still had to mark the list. But the first three days were terrible. I had to force myself, I wanted to quit and went on only because I didn't want to disappoint you.

I: I am glad that you were successful in keeping it up.

S: I am calling you to ask if I really have to try out the other things. I know now that I like to work on the electric train, there still is much to do, and I could work on it occasionally, maybe that alone will help me?

I: I can understand that but do go on the way we have planned our program. You'll have plenty of time to finish the train, but it is possible that some other activities would also give you pleasure, and that's why I'd like you to try them all out. Keep it up, not for my sake, not even for your own sake, but for the sake of Tom.

On the eleventh day Mr. S called about various details—when should he mark the 0, couldn't he skip a day, he was a little tired and didn't think it necessary to go through the list item by item, he was pretty sure which activities interested him and would be helpful in the future. He never mentioned his thoughts or worries concerning his wife.

At the conclusion of the experiment, on the 16th day, Mr. S presented the following list:

Negative early phase	(-2)	-1	0	+1	+2
	(-2)	-1	0	+1	+2
	(-2)	-1	0	+1	+2
	-2	(-1)	0	+1	+2
	-2	-1	0	+1	(+2)
	-2	-1	0	+1	+2
	-2	(-1)	0	+1	+2
	-2	-1	0	+1	(+2)
	-2	-1	0	+1	+2
	(-2)	-1	0	+1	+2
Positive final phase	-2	-1	0	+1	(+2)
	-2	-1	0	+1	(+2)
	-2	-1	0	+1	(+2)
	-2	-1	0	(+1)	+2
	-2	-1	0	+1	(+2)

Process of healing through dereflection

I: Mr. S, I congratulate you on your success. You wouldn't have expected to get that many plus marks, would you?

S: That's right, I never would have thought that possible. Now we know what activities suit me best.

I: We know more than that. Just look at the list. During the past five days you had nothing but pluses. Do you think that was the result of a special activity?

S: What do you mean?

I: Some of the pluses came after working on the train. Others after making a salad, or after working on the stove, or helping Tom with his homework. Did you think of your troubles?

S: Well, I hardly had time for that. Working all day, and doing these things at night, and then scoring them . . .

I: And brooding about your wife, that would have been asking too much, wouldn't it? (We both laugh.) You have gained strength through this program which you carried out so valiantly, Mr. S, a lot of additional strength. You have conquered your trouble! Now let them come, all these thoughts about your wife. Invite the thoughts to visit you at night, they no longer have power over you, you are armed to meet them, you have a whole list of weapons against them. (Using paradoxical intention and reinforcement by suggestion.) Why bother to sit in a corner in despair, overpowered by a sad thought? If you feel like that again, then make one of your magnificent salads, or build a tunnel for your train, or tape-record a program you like, and you will realize how strong you have become, how much inner peace you have gained.

S:　And you think I won't have a relapse?

I:　Oh, you can afford a little relapse, now and then. You have gone through difficult times but you have proven to yourself that you have the strength to overcome them. The suffering you have experienced has made you strong. During the next week try and do what is fun for you, without a schedule or activities, and you will see that you don't have to do things, you can occasionally take a rest without being overwhelmed by troubling thoughts.

In the follow-up session Martin S said that he had overcome his depression even though he had finished the projects that were to guide us in therapy: setting up the train and repairing the stove. By asking him to think of activities that would be a clue to therapy, therapy had become unnecessary. The defiant power of his human spirit had been aroused and helped him find a meaningful direction in his life as a single father.

A young psychiatrist who had observed the case raised the question of whether the success was due to the method of dereflection or my personal caring. I pointed out to her that in logotherapy methods and caring are so interlinked that an either/or question cannot be answered. In dereflection the counselor helps clients find goals or tasks which capture the clients' total attention so they free themselves from a fixed and unhealthy attitude, to a new lifestyle.

DEREFLECTION IN MEDICAL MINISTRY

Dereflection is also applicable where medical help is no longer possible, as in cases of incurable sickness and dying. In the face of death all psychological methods lose their significance. There are few words of comfort a healthy person can say that will reach the dying. But the possibility exists up to the last moment to dereflect the thoughts of the dying from their impending death onto the meanings of their lives, their past accomplishments, which no one can take away from them. Here dereflection is reinforced by a modification of attitudes, away from feelings of futility to those of achievement. In this extreme situation the entire spiritual potential is mobilized so the inexorable fate becomes transformed into a splendid human achievement of which the client can be proud up to the last breath.

Similarly, dereflection can be used for patients who suffer from symptoms whose causes cannot be eliminated, such as some psychoses, attacks of epilepsy, organic deficiencies, and even endogenous depressions. Patients wait for their attacks, constantly observe themselves for signs of symptoms, or are preoccupied with the state of their mood. It is important to counteract this hyperreflection, even when the symptom cannot be removed.

In cases of endogenous depressions Frankl proved that patients may be suffering from what he calls "piggyback depressions," secondary depressions which "ride piggyback" on the primary depression. In such cases the endogenous depression, caused within the patients' physical dimension, is now joined by a second depression that originates in the psyche: the patients are depressed about being depressed. In some cases one can see how patients weep about their tendency to weep, and are sad about their sadness, and thus reinforce their depression. Dereflection enables such patients to at least free themselves from their "superimposed" depression and to reduce their suffering to a level that is unavoidable.

Dereflection, which counters hyperreflection and hyperintention, requires a different plan of treatment than paradoxical intention which counters phobias and obsessive compulsion. Paradoxical intention begins with a self-distancing from one's symptoms, followed by a change of attitude, a reduction of symptoms, and the discovery of meaningful activities and experiences.

In dereflection the fourth step comes much earlier in the treatment. The patients are helped toward finding new life content that dereflects their attention from their unhealthy preoccupation with a problem. But before this goal can be achieved, it is necessary to expand their attention toward a field of meaning potentials beyond their own selves, to arouse their capacity for self-transcendence, the reaching out toward someone to love or a cause to make their own.

If the therapy succeeds in freeing the clients from focusing on themselves and guiding them to a meaningful object outside, the symptoms become more manageable and often disappear. And as soon as the clients have experienced the healing power in self-transcendence, their attitude begins to change.

The four steps of a treatment plan using dereflection, therefore, tend to have a different sequence from that used in paradoxical intention and most other methods of logotherapy:

1. Self-transcendence.
2. Finding meaningful tasks and goals.
3. Reduction of symptoms.
4. Change in attitudes.

Self-transcendence is more than mere dereflection. It presents a direct contrast to that most difficult of all psychological sicknesses, egocentricity. Persons who think of nothing but their own well-being will always detect disturbances and symptoms, and no one will be able to cure them completely. True human happiness lies in the ability to forget oneself. This truth is hard to communicate to today's men and women who are inclined to be self-centered. That makes dereflection one of the most difficult, yet most important, therapeutic methods.

Case # 29:

I once had a patient who was on a visit from a distant city and could stay in Munich for only a few days. She suffered from a variety of disturbances such as self-doubt, anxiety, and despondency. In the ten therapy sessions at our disposal she talked exclusively about herself. Not a word about her husband and children, not a word about general or professional subjects, nothing but, "I, I, I . . ." She displayed a tremendous amount of self-pity, everything upset her, nothing was good enough for her, other people paid too little attention to her, no one really understood her, therapists had failed her, and she expected no help from me either. Of her husband she said, "I am afraid he will die before I have enough love and affection from him."

So much egoism is tragic. A person so much concerned with herself must succumb to despair.

In our few hours I fought for one thing only: her self-transcendence. Her position was, "You are here for me. You must help me." Slowly and cautiously I tried to guide her to ask herself the questions: "And for whom am *I* here? Whom can *I* help?" When she didn't see the significance of these questions I shocked her by ignoring her doubts and anxieties. I concentrated on helping her gain a perspective that would take her at least one step beyond herself and bring others into her field of vision. The time was too short to see definite results. I only hope that the switch rail I set in her thinking will lead her in a new direction.

Dereflection is extremely difficult to achieve in our time when egocentricity has become so dominant. But all the more important is its place in today's psychotherapy. One can almost judge the degree of health in patients by the extent to which they talk about their problems. When they get to the point where they resist the therapy and say, "I have no time (or desire) to talk about my silly symptoms," they are on the way to recovery. The psychological crisis will last as long as they find the time and the desire to think about their health.

Such considerations lead to serious conclusions about psychotherapy in general. It is in the nature of psychotherapy to focus the patients' attention—whether on purpose or not—on their symptoms. The unavoidable concern of the therapist with the patients' sickness is enough to heighten their emphasis of it and prompt them to reflect on it. When they have to take medication three times a day, they have to remember to take it and are thus reminded that they are different from other people who don't have to take medication. Any medical treatment at first increases the patients' focus on their sickness.

I am convinced that it ought to be the primary goal of any treatment to stop and counteract the patients' preoccupation with their sickness. This needs to be done not only where the technique of dereflection is directed at a specific goal, like overcoming impotence, but as a principle of general dereflection.

General dereflection is not aimed at helping patients find new meaning possibilities in order to reduce an unfortunate hyper-reflection (as for instance by means of an alternate list). It is aimed at gradually reducing the importance patients attach to their problems because other things and people outside themselves have come into view and are important. The patients' goal is "to get well by finding meaning." The therapist's goal is to "to make well by dereflection."

Psychoanalysis treats causes to reduce symptoms. Behavior therapy and logotherapy treat symptoms, without necessarily looking into causes. General dereflection goes beyond the treatment of symptoms. It approaches a "therapy of the person from the ground up"—not by unearthing deep-seated causes, but by reducing the influence of causes and symptoms. When symptoms and psychological causes become unimportant, they continue to exist but do no harm and, having lost their power, they fade away.

General dereflection is thus a third possibility dealing with the cause-symptom chain. It is an approach still to be explored, only hinted at in the writings of Frankl.

To Case #8:

The woman who felt her husband did not understand her paid a great deal of attention to all the daily events that made her feel misunderstood, neglected, or isolated. In every incident she looked for negative interpretations; the smallest discomfort was eagerly noted. After the therapy had eliminated minor marital conflicts and somewhat raised her level of tolerance for the trifling troubles with her neighbors, other little "problems" came to the fore: a bad reaction to certain TV programs, a distaste for a bad odor from a nearby canal, sleep disturbances during her period, unhappiness with housework. All these "symptoms" could be treated singly but I realized that it was her basic attitude that continuously produced new reflections on "sicknesses," and that this attitude resisted all therapeutic attempts.

I had worked out a rather complicated therapy plan when chance came to my rescue. Near her home there was a camp for Vietnamese refugees. When she told me about it with some interest, I suggested she might inquire at the camp office if assistance from the neighboring community would be welcome.

She took the suggestion and became busy organizing a collection and the distribution of gifts. She made peace with her neighbors while asking them for used toys for the children in the camp. When she came to our sessions, she told me about her new volunteer activities, and I waited for new emotional complications. None came. The woman had become well.

Such instances where chance plays the part of the "therapist" are not rare and should make us take notice. All those annoyances the patient complained about still existed but they had become unimportant compared to her new self-chosen task. They did not receive any attention and faded away.

General dereflection may have many applications beyond the patient-therapist situation. Obese persons, for instance, who are on a diet, have their attention focused on their weight which they check daily. This hyperreflection may be the reason these dietary cures seldom have lasting success. If overweight people would redirect their attention to, say, gardening that needs to be done before the onset of winter, it might happen that they would "forget" some meals and lose some weight. This approach may seem to run counter to the fashionable cry for self-actualization, but it could well be the way out from a dead-end in therapy.

COMBINATION METHODS

Both dereflection and paradoxical intention can break an unwanted behavior pattern in which clients feel trapped. Both methods make them aware, if only for a moment, that they are not victims but masters of this pattern.

To decide which of the two methods is most applicable, the counselor must distinguish between cases dealing with abnormal conditions, which the client fears (stuttering, excessive sweating), or normal conditions which the client wants to force (sleep, orgasm).

Abnormal conditions which the clients fear are best treated with paradoxical intention. For normal conditions which are blocked by hyperreflection, dereflection is indicated. The following table illustrates the applicability:

Paradoxical intention ⟶	prevents ⟶	an event or a condition (fear)
Dereflection ⟶	brings about ⟶	an event or a condition (sleep)
Change of attitude ⟶	helps master ⟶	an event or a condition (incurable sickness)
Self-detachment ⟶	helps apply ⟶	paradoxical intention
Self-transcendence ⟶	helps apply ⟶	dereflection
(Auto) suggestion ⟶	helps bring about ⟶	change of attitudes

In cases where a combination of both methods is indicated, it is better to liberate the client first from the grip of anticipatory anxiety (through paradoxical intention), and then to remove the blockage of hyperreflection (through dereflection). The following case will illustrate how the combination may be applied.

Case #30:

Mrs. F had been suffering for years from a severe phobia of air trams. Her husband was a photographer specializing in mountain views. They used their vacations to ride up the mountains for spectacular views and motifs, taking various air-tramways or gondolas to reach the heights. Mrs. F actually loved to accompany her husband because she enjoyed arranging photos for calendars, but she had a phobia about using the floating cabins. She didn't mind the chair lift as much because in it she felt less closed in, and the trips were less steep than those using large cabins with many people.

Formerly she had gone up on foot and met her husband, who used the air-tram, on top of the mountain. But gradually she found the hike too strenuous. She had gone to psychiatrists for years and tried out all kinds of medication. One of them enabled her to use the air-tram once in a while, enduring palpitations and dizziness, closing her eyes and holding on tightly to her husband. Mrs. F came to my office in January and confessed that she was already dreading the thought of summer and wondered whether she wouldn't do well to just remain home while her husband went on his mountain trips. I offered a counter-suggestion. Since we couldn't practice our therapy out there in nature, she might try something in town. During this half year before the summer season I would train her to use some techniques so she would find it unnecessary to visit a psychotherapist again; she herself would be able to overcome her fear.

We used our time well. In all sorts of enclosed car and train situations we kept practicing paradoxical intention. A bus became an air tram and Mrs. F worked on progressive muscle relaxation combined with elements of autogenic training; one variant was used for quick relaxation. Then we worked out little tasks to do to keep busy in a closed area, such as difficult crossword puzzles and writing letters. We went on short stretches sitting in a streetcar and she chose the appropriate reaction to use as we covered distances connected with mountain areas in our imagination.

Work Agreement. Together we take a train.

Question: How will you use your time before entering the mountain train?

Answer: I resolve firmly to enter this contraption with immense heart palpitations. After all, I want a little excitement for my money.

Question: What about your eyes?

Answer: Of course, they'll be open, otherwise I would miss the opportunity to get the most beautiful attack of dizziness. It's like being dizzy from champagne, I tell you!

(We enter the train and sit in our compartment.)

Question: That's a bad time, this waiting, isn't it?

Answer: Oh, not at all. I have my book of puzzles to keep me busy. I made a bet with my husband that this puzzle will be finished without any errors when we get to the top. He doesn't believe me, but I'll show him. The winner of the bet gets a silver pin: he for his cap, or I for my jacket.

(The train starts moving. She works on her crossword puzzle.)

Question: This air train is getting a little shaky and you're starting to feel that funny feeling; will fear take over?

Answer: Fear won't take over; it would like to, but it won't succeed. See, I have something I can do against this funny feeling: I'll clench my fists, tense up, and hold the tension—slowly relax, enjoy the feeling of relaxation—enjoy it a little more now and feel restfulness and relaxation going through both hands. Next, I press the knees tightly together, still tighter, just a little more—

and now relax the knees, that's pleasant, I can feel the warmth in my knees—this warmth envelops my whole body—and now I breathe deeply, breathe in, hold it, hold my breath—and slowly breathe out—feels good, this sense of relaxation and feeling the warmth and peacefulness—it breathes me, quietly and evenly, quietly-evenly am I being breathed through—no effort— enjoying the relaxation—relaxing even more deeply—and now if I look at the crossword puzzle I feel fine again—I come up with a solution—I'm looking right now!

Question: We're arriving at the mountain station. You put the puzzle book away. What now?

Answer: I feel proud. I'm filled with pride. I can look through the window. I am here on top. I can take it, come what may. Let the whole contraption fall into the abyss, I dared look out the window. I really made it all by myself, I dared it and made it. Let the whole gondola spin around its axis—that would be fun. I look out the window in spite of my fear.

(The train stops at the station and we step out.)

Question: Now you are getting out of the air tram. Couldn't you get a little scared now that it is over? Just a tiny weensy bit?

Answer: I left the fear in the gondola. Why should I take it along? Some other passenger may want it, make friends with it. The gondola is still here and did not fall down. My heart is still here and didn't explode. Too bad, I would have liked some excitement. Nothing ever happens on these trips. Oh dear—now I remember: I didn't finish my puzzle. Well, I can work on it some more on our return trip. I'm looking forward to it. But the pin goes to my husband. Shucks!

In this case the following methods were employed:
Medication, beforehand.
Paradoxical intention (before possible anticipatory anxiety).
Dereflection (to bridge difficult time spans).
Self-relaxation (in emergencies).
Activating the defiant power (at a point of relatively high security).
Reward: Pride in accomplishment.
Paradoxical intention again: to avoid relapses.
In between, repeated distancing of self from her fear.

Armed thus, our patient went on her vacation. After a week I received a postcard with a lovely mountain motif. "Dear Dr. Lukas: I finished the crossword puzzle, and before I begin flirting with my fear, I'm writing you a few lines. Yes, I'm writing you from this air tram, writing on my husband's back, with my eyes open. He can hardly believe it. Isn't that something? Aren't you surprised, too?"

HYPERREFLECTION AND MEDICATION

Hyperreflection may also present a problem when, in the course of the therapy, medication is used to stabilize the patient. When medication is withdrawn, patients often suffer relapses, and not just because the pharmaceutical effect has ended. Two kinds of withdrawal symptoms come into play: a physiological withdrawal symptom because a chemical dependency was established, and a psychogenic withdrawal symptom because patients, after medication has ended, may observe themselves anxiously (hyperreflection) to see how they feel without the medication, which produces anticipatory anxiety and opens the way for the relapse.

To avoid the consequences of a sudden termination of medication, it is possible nowadays to manufacture pills which look alike but contain different amounts of the medication. In the course of the therapy, patients can be given pills which contain less and less of the medication without their being aware of the reduction from, say, 40 percent to 0 percent (placebo). When the use of pills is discontinued, the patients are told that for the past two weeks they have taken only placebos which proves that they no longer need medication. This gradual reduction minimizes the physiological as well as the psychogenic consequences of the withdrawal because the patients now realize that they have felt good although they have swallowed only sugar during the past two weeks.

Suggestion plays its part in therapy, even if suggestions are only implied. Ineffective medication (placebo) may have positive results, and the sudden termination of superfluous medication may affect patients negatively. The therapist must always consider the feedback mechanism and its effect on the patients. She must also take into account the dimension of the human spirit by summoning its resources, including decision making, responsibleness, and the will to meaning.

Whatever one may say about the techniques of logotherapy, one thing is certain: it is not persuasion. The more the therapist tries to persuade patients to change their attitude about a problem, the more they are likely to defend their identity within their condition of illness. Any persuasion only reinforces the resistance against a moving away from the symptoms.

EXPANDING THE MEANING HORIZON

An unhealthy hyperreflection is dereflected to a specific healthy target—the impotent man to his partner; the depressed Mr. S to his list of fifteen activities; the phobic Mrs. F to her crossword puzzles. Behind the specific targets that patients choose according to *their* preferences lies a general expansion of their meaning horizon. Nothing protects a person from neuroses, psychoses, depressions, and psychosomatic illnesses as much as a task, a goal that can pull the patient from sickness to health. In a Socratic dialogue the logotherapist can elucidate a variety of activities and experiences—work, play, hobbies, sports, art, friendship, family—which the patient found meaningful in the past and has now forgotten, ignored, or discarded as no longer applicable; or, equally important, the therapist may help patients think of activities and experiences that have appeal to them for the future but are rejected right now as hopeless. A widening of the meaning horizon is often the most solid foundation for therapy.

A warning: Activities ordinarily helpful in expanding meaning possibilities may have the opposite effect. One-sided activities may threaten meaning orientation. A woman who spends all her time washing, ironing, cooking, cleaning, and sewing for her big family is highly active, yet may be frustrated. If she were to find the time to read a book, give a party, take a hike, or go to the theatre, her domestic duties would give her more joy. Overdemands *and* underdemands are dangerous and unhealthy. A wide field of activities and experiences is like a life belt that keeps us afloat and protects us from drowning in existential frustration; but it must not be so heavy that it sinks us.

When during the logotherapeutic recovery process patients gain new attitudes toward their situation and life in general, they experience such a positive feedback that they become receptive to a widened meaning orientation. The therapist gradually becomes superfluous. The clients—no longer "patients"—take over their lives enriched in values and meanings. The logotherapeutic dialogue has ended successfully. The clients have reached their goal, the therapist has nothing to add and quietly steps back. In this common effort the patients must give their trust but the therapists must give their all. It is not enough for therapists to be good psychologists, or even good psychotherapists. They must remain human beings. Logotherapy is an encounter between two human beings. As Frankl has shown, it represents the rehumanization of psychotherapy.

7

The Application Of
The Appealing Technique

The appealing technique rests, as with all other logotherapeutic methods, on trust in the human being.

It is amazing that logotherapy has developed when trust in human nature is shaken, when people question everything including themselves, when values and traditions crumble and uncertainty sweeps over us. Science presents human nature in mechanistic-functional terms, yet a therapy was born that pictures the essence of human nature in terms of dignity, responsibleness, and meaning orientation.

For half a century scientists have established, and correctly, our dependence on childhood experiences, social environment, conscious and unconscious drives, and education. There is danger in this trend to scientific determinism. Logotherapy has consistently warned against it and directed attention to the human spirit. It insists that the defiant power of the spirit enables us to confront existing influences, even blows of fate.

Logotherapy appeals to our defiant power through the three methods discussed—modification of attitudes, paradoxical intention, and dereflection. Some people, as stated before, are too weak to respond to these methods, and for these a special appealing technique has been developed. Because a significant group of people who can benefit from this technique are drug addicts I shall discuss the appealing method as it applies to this group.

Much of drug addiction derives from such negative factors as poor living conditions, parental example, environment, or peer pressure. Emphasizing these negative factors allows young people to disregard their capacity to resist these influences and to believe that, under certain conditions, they are bound to become addicts. Logotherapy cautions against such reductionism and determinism.

113

We cannot lead a meaningful life if we see ourselves as "nothing but" products of outside influences, as creatures in search of temporary pleasure.

There is also a danger in the opposite direction: "positive" factors, too, may lead to a lack of meaning. An abundance of consumer goods, unrestricted freedom to do and choose, a great amount of leisure also lead to inner emptiness and a desperate search for meaning.

Both deprivation and superabundance are dangerous. Deprivation may be more dangerous on the biological level, but superabundance is a greater threat psychologically. Deprived persons can find meaning in setting themselves the task of overcoming their miserable situation, but abundance offers, to begin with, no aims to reach for. Aimlessness can lead to existential frustration which is the breeding ground for suicide, crime, sexual perversion, and drug use. Frustrated people desperately search for an aim—or the illusion of an aim.

TWO TYPES OF ADDICTION

On illusions brought about by drugs Frankl writes: "A man who tries to anaesthetize himself solves no problem, eliminates no misfortune. What he eliminates is merely the consequence of the misfortune—his feeling of unhappiness. But just as we cannot create something by looking at it, so we cannot destroy it by looking away."

Frankl referred here to cases of addiction caused, or at least triggered, by some event. A man may turn to alcohol after a failure in his profession, or a woman may start taking sleeping pills after her child dies. The temporary dulling of the pain does not change the situation, however. Such people escape reality for a while, but reality still exists.

The more they escape reality, the weaker their strength to bear it. The drug undermines their defiant power, weakens their willpower, clouds their responsibility, and destroys their freedom to make choices. It blocks their human dimension and, once this happens, they really are victims of reduction. They are reduced to persons controlled by the amount of the drugs in their blood. They now are indeed "nothing but" a conditioned organism full of automatic reflexes. They are lowered to a subhuman level, no longer searching for meanings, values and goals, but blindly obeying the dictates of their urges. They are the slaves of desire, ruled by hunger for the drug and by fear of their withdrawal pain.

Addictions triggered by a specific cause used to be the rule. But now we encounter a new type of neurosis and a new type of addiction. One might call it "noogenic" addiction. People, especially the young, become addicted without a cause. They come from well-to-do families, are raised in comfort—even luxury—in an atmosphere of caring. Suddenly they take to stimulants and hallucinogens.

No cause? There *is* a cause that is not as obvious as a blow of fate: a feeling of meaninglessness. A blow of fate causes distress, and distress challenges us to come to grips with it and possibly overcome it. It probes our strength. But a feeling of meaninglessness causes emptiness, boredom, indifference. We don't need the resources of our spirit if nothing is worth the effort. Nietzsche said, "He who has a Why to live for can bear almost any What." Logotherapy adds, "He who has no Why to live for is unable to enjoy any What."

In sum: The major motivation in drugs is the attempt to numb the pain caused by a distressing event or to find illusions that will fill an empty and boring life. Both distress and boredom are temptations to flee reality. To be sure, there are other superficial causes such as curiosity, enticement by others, revolt against authority, example, naiveté, misinformation, as well as poor living conditions, marriage problems, school stress, and others. But these do not strike at the core of the problem.

PRACTICAL APPLICATIONS

Logotherapy by itself is not sufficient in drug treatment; it is complementary. One could say that logotherapy will not cure drug addiction. But no cure is complete without logotherapy.

It is hopeless to get severe alcoholics to rediscover new goals in life because they have only one goal: alcohol. Therapy must begin by removing the physiological and psychological blocks that prevent patients from reaching the resources of their spirit. This is why treatment must first concentrate on pharmaceutical and psychological help.

Once patients are detoxified their willpower and their freedom to make decisions are restored. They become open to exploring meaning possibilities and seeking new directions. But it would be a mistake to stop therapy at this point. What happens if the "cured" addicts are released from the clinic with their blood analysis normal and an inculcated aversion to drugs but are full of anxiety, doubts, and frustration, guilt feelings about the past and uncertainty about the future? Such patients will be hit by existential distress of which they had not even been aware during their addiction. They will face the question what the treatment was for, what meaning their future holds, and how their past experiences fit into the present. At this point therapy is needed that dares to enter the dimension of the spirit and to take part in the patients' pursuit of meaning—therapy that can assist in finding a new attitude toward living. In this phase logotherapy is indispensable.

When drug patients return to their old surroundings after their cure, confront their daily problems, and still carry the same feeling of emptiness, they become doubly doubtful about the meaning of it all. They have been through failures, addiction, horror trips, breakdowns, clinics and attempts to get hold of themselves. If they are now overwhelmed by the thought that "all this is useless, my life is messed up," a relapse is unavoidable.

Logotherapy is flexible and can be combined with other forms of therapy. Frankl tells of a combined therapy for a depressed patient, which applies to cases of drug addiction.

A woman suffered from periodic endogenous depression. For the endogenic (organic) component of her sickness she received medication. But she also had a psychogenic disturbance because she was desperate about her continuous weepy condition, and for this she needed psychotherapeutic treatment. Frankl tried to help her see that fighting an organically caused depression was useless and advised her to let the depression pass like a cloud over the sun. After the passing of her depressive phase she would again have access to the joys of life.

When her depression faded and the psychological blocks gradually dissolved, her spiritual distress and frustration rose to the surface. She now suffered because she felt her life was meaningless as a woman condemned to repeated attacks of depression. Now Frankl applied logotherapy proper. Through extended Socratic (self-finding) dialogues she learned to see that her life, in spite of repeated depressions, was full of personal tasks and challenges, including the challenge to triumph over her physiologically caused depression. Her defiant power was activated to help her discover a personal life that was meaningful even if she still suffered from attacks of depression.

What is true for the endogenously depressed is also true for drug addicts: As long as they are in the grip of total dependence on the drug, their horizon is not wide enough for a Socratic dialogue in search of personal meanings. But after medical help has weakened the biological and psychological dependence, the dialogue can lay the foundations for a new and healthy life that will protect the patients against a relapse into despair and drugs. In this sense logotherapy is complementary *and* preventive therapy.

A TWO-STEP APPROACH

In my practice I send drug-dependent patients to a detoxification clinic. At the same time I offer them logotherapy as a follow-up treatment. Physiological help is a precondition for successful logotherapy.

My follow-up treatment is done in two steps: the first is on a psychological level; the second enters the dimension of the spirit. But even during the psychological phase I prepare the conditions for a Socratic dialogue that will explore meaning possibilities.

During the first phase I use relaxation exercises (autogenic training, progressive relaxation according to Jacobson, or meditation exercises) by getting the patients to listen to cassette tapes. As soon as they are able to manage their physical relaxation, I add suggestive training of the will as a transition to the logotherapeutic dialogue (see page 00).

The sequence is:

Pre-logotherapeutic step in the clinic: Biological detoxification.
First step in the logotherapeutic follow-up: Psychological relaxation exercises.
(Transition: Suggestive training of the will)
Second step in the logotherapeutic follow-up: Socratic dialogue to explore meaning possibilities.

I always let the patients take the taped exercises home. This is useful for all unstable patients. As long as these patients are with the therapist in an atmosphere of caring, understanding, security, and patience, they find it relatively easy to relax, have good intentions, and imagine new beginnings. As soon as they are home, alone, facing the normal demands of life, anxiety rises, the relaxation is over, intentions fade, and beginnings look more doubtful than ever. It would be too much to expect under such circumstances for them to lie down and do the exercises from memory. This would require more self-discipline, willpower, and strength of concentration than they can muster.

It is an enormous advantage if the patients have a cassette to which they can listen while relaxing. The cassette brings back the voice of the therapist, spares them the necessity to think, and enables them to surrender to the suggestive effect of soothing formulations.

The technique has another advantage: the addicts are accustomed to artificial means to change their moods. Deprived of one means they are now offered another in the form of a cassette. They are suggestible (a danger); but used here to strengthen their stability, the words of the therapist gradually become their conviction.

Case # 31:

A young woman, mother of five small children, started to take more and more sleeping pills since her husband was taken to prison. When her neighbors heard the children cry one whole afternoon, they called the police who broke the door open and found the woman lying unconscious on her bed. The children were placed temporarily with neighbors while she was placed in a clinic. After her release she was told that in case of a relapse the children would be taken away from her. She swore she would kill herself if this happened. She was sent to our counseling center for follow-up treatment.

During the initial sessions it became clear that she took sleeping pills when she was seized by worries about the future of her family (justified with her husband in prison) or when she was upset with her children (unavoidable with five small children). She became tense, could not relax, had trouble falling asleep, and took the tablets. It was an ideal case for relaxation exercises. After she had mastered them well I added formulations of suggestive training of the will. The text went along these lines:

1. Normal relaxation formulations, similar to progressive relaxation.

2. Suggestive training of the will (spoken quietly and suggestively, with pauses in between):

You are now in a condition of complete relaxation—you become calmer and calmer—you feel an inner peace and contentment. You only hear my voice—nothing else can penetrate to you. You may hear outside noises but they don't bother you. You are completely calm and relaxed—all tension is gone—all anxiety has left you—you hear some noises—but nothing disturbs you.

Your arms and legs are heavy and warm—heavy and warm. You don't want to move them—all is calm within—pleasantly calm and quiet.

You are in a condition of complete relaxation—and out of this inner calm—you collect your thoughts—concentrate your thoughts—listen to thoughts that come to you—feel the heaviness of your body—the warmth that engulfs you—listen to your thoughts—which no longer slip away—which no longer deal with the small concerns of daily life—all is far away—they do not matter—only your thoughts matter—they form themselves—to a firm will—you remain completely calm and relaxed—nothing can bother you—the tension is gone—listen to your thoughts—concentrate on your firm will—you feel the experience of your willing—you will—you want—you want to remain well.

You think of nothing but of your will—all your thoughts are centered on your will.

You want to remain well.

Breathe calmly—regularly—calmly and relaxed—all anxiety is gone—nothing can disturb you. You feel the calm and warmth which surrounds you—and protects you—feel the heaviness of your body—concentrate your thoughts a little more—on your will to remain well—hold on to this will—hold on firmly—don't let your thoughts slip away.

You want to remain well.

Hold on strongly to this firm will—very firmly.

You want to remain well.

You *can* remain well—your own will holds you up firmly—very firmly.

And now breathe in deeply—breathe out deeply—in and out—

you may let your thoughts go now—you need not concentrate any longer—gradually bring your thoughts back to your surroundings. Remain calm and relaxed—free from the worries of every-day life. You are joyful and content—joyful and content.

3. Waking.

You are now completely calm and relaxed. Enjoy the beautiful calmness and warmth of your body. When I say "Now!" open your eyes, look around the room and feel fresh and wide awake. When I say "Now!" your mind will again be alert and active—you can stand with all your strength in the middle of reality.

Now!

Now you are wide awake, happy, and ready to go. Your firm will and your inner peace will accompany you during the day. Remain sitting for a while until you are ready.

The training is concluded.

The woman got used to the cassette tapes (I had given her four different tapes of varying length and intensity) and she stated that the tapes helped her more than the valium. She also received a special tape to help her fall asleep. On this tape the waking instruction was replaced by a "posthypnotic order" to reach out and turn the cassette off and to sleep well till morning when she would open her eyes and feel fresh and alive, armed with a firm will and an inner peace that would stay with her all day. Whenever she felt she was getting upset she put on one of the tapes and regained her composure.

All this was, of course, no great success in itself. It was merely a switch to a more harmless method of helping her than taking sleeping pills. But it worked in the long run, and even when she did not fall asleep but merely calmed down, she was better able to take care of her children than when she was under the influence of tranquilizers.

As a next step I instructed her to gradually reduce the volume of the tapes so she could become increasingly independent of them and gather her own willpower to apply to her daily life.

Since she now had a stronger willpower, she was to test it on some situations of daily living. We went through experiences that in the past had upset her and discussed how they could be handled in a more positive manner. For instance, when her baby boy refused to eat his cereal and threw it on the floor, she was to calmly take his plate away, clean him up and take him to the playroom without giving him any more food until the next meal. Through these practical exercises she learned to remain calm and consistent, and not to dramatize these minor irritations. Her new behavior pattern reduced the danger of a relapse.

One day she told me proudly that she no longer needed the cassettes. She was able to lie down, calm down, and "feel her firm will," as she put it. She had become more stable and ready for the logotherapeutic dialogue. Together we considered what she could do for her family and herself to meet her self-chosen tasks in a more positive mood. Her most important task was to bring up her five children so they would be healthy and happy, and also to help her husband adjust after his release from prison and gain a firm footing. We eventually agreed that it would be best to place her three small children in a day-care center while the two others were in school, so she could earn money in cleaning jobs. She found work with a construction firm which, as chance would have it, had openings for unskilled laborers. After she had worked for a while and proved to be reliable and hardworking she asked the boss to give her husband a chance after his release from prison.

A year later I ran into her in a grocery store, two children on one hand and a full shopping bag in the other. Both she and her husband worked for the construction firm, and neither had had a relapse. Her husband no longer took to stealing and she no longer took valium. "The children sense it too," she told me, "that we are okay. We are now saving for a used car. Won't it be fun when we can drive to the country and have a picnic? I still use your cassette in emergencies but I really believe I can manage without it. I have more willpower; I'm not so easily upset."

During the first phase of the appealing technique, by using relaxation exercises and cassettes, the patients are calmed, gain distance from their upsets, and learn to use their willpower to get rid of anxieties, tensions, and nightmares; because, similar to paradoxical intention, relaxation and emotional upsets cancel each other out.

AUTOGENIC TRAINING

If patients have experience in autogenic training, the therapist may add formulations to strengthen their will or to guide them to a more positive attitude to life, both logotherapeutic goals. Though still working from the dimension of the psyche, we try to activate the resources of the spirit by positive feedback effect.

This version of autogenic training consists of a preparatory phase, the use of formulations given in a rhythm of about a minute each, and a wakening.

Preparation:

Please lie down so you feel comfortable, and close your eyes. Surrender to the calm and relaxation which flows through you and fills you. Nothing disturbs you. Thoughts rise up in you and pass by you. All your worries and problems are far away; they are unimportant. You feel nothing but a deep inner stillness which gives you strength and courage to live. You lie quietly, you are relaxed, nothing disturbs you, my voice is of no importance. Only *your* will and *your* concentration bring about the deep, inner peace that fills you completely.

Formulations (one minute apart):

I am calm, completely calm. I am calm, completely calm.

Arms and legs are heavy, very heavy, arms and legs are heavy.

Arms and legs are warm, very warm, arms and legs are warm.

I am calm, very calm. I am calm.

My forehead is pleasantly cool, my forehead is pleasantly cool.

I am calm, very calm. I am calm.

Now I can concentrate, I concentrate now—very intensively—on one thought, I concentrate now—very intensively—on one thought.

More and more willpower, more and more willpower.

I feel calm, heavy and warm, calm, heavy, and warm.

I am calm, very calm. I am calm.

Waking:

We now conclude the training, we now conclude the training. Please breathe deeply, and once more breathe deeply. Now make fists, tighten your muscles in your upper arm and move your arms quickly. Lift your arms, stretch your arms, bend your arms and relax. Do this several times. Now lift your upper body, very slowly, into a sitting position. We shall now count slowly backwards from 4 to 1, and when we get to 1 open your eyes and feel refreshed and wide awake! The inner peace will be with you all day long. We now count: 4—3—2—1—open your eyes! Remain sitting for a little while until you are completely composed. The training is concluded.

It has been found beneficial for this version of autogenic training to use only the first three of the regular seven formulations: calmness, heaviness, warmth, and possibly coolness of the forehead. Otherwise the exercise becomes too long, too diverse, and often too intensive. We don't need to bring about a heavy hypnotic condition, only a deep calming at the threshold of consciousness where the formulations are still accessible to the mind.

Those who wish to work with this method must get thorough training and information on where it is indicated or counterindicated, about application methods, dangers, and medical implications. It is irresponsible and dangerous to apply suggestive methods without proper training.

For any suggestive method the following five rules are useful:

1. If both therapist and patient are of the same sex, the voice of the therapist can be used to help patients identify the voice with their own thoughts. In such cases the pertinent formulations should be spoken in the I-form to assist identification. If therapist and patient are of different sexes, a light transference is used to bring about suggestion by using the You-form. (For the woman in Case #31 I chose the You-form because she was insecure, easily suggestible, and I suspected she would react better to my "orders" than to her own intentions. Later I noticed that she also could react well to the I-form. The more self-assurance she gained the more I freed her from my influence and let her stand on her own).

2. As a rule of thumb, the intervals should be about a minute, adjusted to the individual patient. Patients who can easily turn off their thoughts and are not tortured by painful thoughts, can be given longer intervals to become relaxed. Those, however, who during the intervals become restless or begin to brood, must be given, at least at first, shorter intervals. The length of the intervals is adjusted step by step according to the patients' reaction.

3. The formulations must be genuine, simple, and impressive. What is important to me is to incorporate logotherapeutic ideas that cannot be readily communicated to patients when access to their spirit is blocked. The suggestions contain positive and hopeful ideas and, through feedback reaction, help restore the patients' health.

4. The waking must be sufficiently strong. Every relaxation has consequences on the physical level. It's not "just a game and imagination." It can affect the heart, muscles, circulation and other parts of the body. The therapist must make sure that ambulatory patients are fit to be sent off after awakening. If the wakening is not sufficient or is incorrect, patients may be confused for a long time and stagger around. They may fall down the stairs or be hit by a car.

5. Blood pressure must be checked occasionally. During the relaxation blood rises to the surface ("warmth") while the temperature inside the body drops. This may lower blood pressure. If blood pressure was low to begin with, a further drop may cause a collapse when the patient gets up.

The question has been raised whether suggestions contained in the appealing technique do not restrict patients' freedom because they are "talked into something." We must not forget, however, that this first step in the appealing technique represents a transition from complete dependency on the drug to complete restoration of freedom of will. During this transition period one must not make too high a demand on the patients' ability to achieve self-distancing and self-transcendence.

In several cases, I have achieved, through a suggestive training of the will, a genuine strengthening of the will. The patients become convinced that they could concentrate better and persevere. This conviction opened the way to their cure.

THE SECOND PHASE

After the relaxation exercises, the second phase of the follow-up treatment of drug addicts can begin: The logotherapeutic Socratic dialogue aimed at helping the patients find meaning in their lives. The dialogues for drug addicts don't differ from those for other patients who need a strengthening of their meaning orientation.

Again it must be stressed that meaning cannot be "prescribed" by the therapist, but must be found by the patients. They themselves must discover their possibilities, tasks, and goals; they must be aware of their value priorities and learn to live toward whatever they consider worth living for. The therapist can challenge them, involve them in Socratic dialogue, point out meaning possibilities and help them make lists of such possibilities, but the decision is the patients'. First, the former drug addicts must say "yes" to their lives; then they will find their particular place for fulfillment and satisfaction.

After a successful first phase of the follow-up treatment, the logotherapist is in a better starting position for an in-depth dialogue than would have been possible immediately after detoxification. Good intentions are not enough. The addicts had them before but were not able to carry them out. This time it's different. Through training the will, they gain the conviction of more inner strength than ever before, and thus a greater chance to succeed. Even when upset again by restlessness and uneasiness, they can help themselves with the relaxation exercises. They are better equipped to stand up against their own weaker self.

What I try to reduce in the logotherapeutic dialogue is the patients' self-pity which is like a whirlpool dragging them down into hopelessness. Self-pity can express itself in many forms: as a raging against fate (why me?); as a blaming of parents or society for everything that goes wrong; as complaints and as resignation (all is useless); or as a harmful form of dissatisfaction, not one that challenges the undesirable situation but one that saps all strength. Self-pity is extremely dangerous. It does no good for the psychotherapist to show understanding because this will only intensify the self-pity. The therapist must try for a modification of attitudes by showing the patients that unhappy childhood experiences, professional or human failures, or a current crisis provide the chance for a remarkable human achievement—to build up a full and valuable life in spite of everything.

If all goes well in our lives, if our parental home has given us a good start, if we have been granted a fortunate disposition, and have met understanding and help, it is easy to be happy, successful, and satisfied. The more difficult our starting point, the more reason we have to be proud of every small success achieved by our own efforts.

This pride in achievements in spite of obstacles prevents relapses. Logotherapy helps drug addicts break their dependency in two ways: their dependency on the drug and their dependency on their past and "circumstances." As long as the patients say, "Be-

cause my parents didn't want me and didn't care about me I took the wrong turn," they'll be stuck on the wrong turn. Only when they have the courage to say, "*Although* my parents didn't care about me, I'll lead a decent life," will the wrong turn let them go.

The defiant power of the spirit is an enormous reservoir of energy available to patients. If the therapist can help former addicts integrate their negative past into a meaningful present, make the patients see meaning retroactively, the negative past can be overcome. It is well-known how conscientiously ex-addicts help other addicts. It gives them the feeling that they have found a task that enables them to put their unfortunate experiences to use. They are uniquely qualified because they know better than anyone else how addicts feel; they understand the misery of addiction better than the therapist. There was meaning in their suffering. They are proud of their responsibility of working with other addicts, and this helps them remain stable.

The therapeutic chance to find meaning retroactively by learning from mistakes and helping others who are about to make the same mistakes, also exists in criminal psychology. Reformed criminals may regard their past lives as "wasted," which discourages them from going straight. If they are asked to help others go straight, they will see that they are better accepted by criminals because they know their language, their tricks, and their attitudes. They come to see a meaning behind their own experiences.

I often turn to my former drug patients and ask them to help me persuade new addict clients to go to a detoxification clinic. I willingly admit that they are more successful than I am. They feel useful and needed, and it is moving to see how persistently they work on the "new ones." Patients have to feel they are needed—in life and by life, in their society and by their society. To quote Nietzsche again: "He who has a Why to live for can bear almost any What."

I would like to conclude this discussion of logotherapeutic techniques with a caution: More important than any technique is the therapist's personal conviction that the patients will succeed in building, from the wreckage of their past, a new, meaningful, and happy future. The unlimited trust in the human being which characterizes logotherapeutic theory must be present in every single encounter. Patients must sense the trust of the therapist, and it is sometimes enough if *one* person believes in them to prevent a relapse into addiction, sickness, and despair.

In logotherapy the words of the Swiss educator Johann Pestalozzi are pertinent: "You must love people if you wish to change them."

8

The "Ideal" Logotherapist

I have often asked myself what the qualifications are for a "good" logotherapist. Am I a good logotherapist?

The darkness of prevailing meaninglessness, dissatisfaction, and disorientation frightens me. But should logotherapists permit themselves to be frightened? Shouldn't we be on a "higher" (healthy) level, above doubt and despair, guiding people toward a fulfilled life? But if therapists are in that position, can we still bend down and pull up those unhappy people and hold them securely? Or would the distance be too great, the help too remote?

It is difficult for a healthy person to help the sick with comforting words because the sick will say to themselves, "It's easy for them to talk, they are not sick." Are good logotherapists, then, people who must themselves wrestle with meanings and share their doubts with their patients? If they do that, will they not transmit uncertainty and despondency, and discourage their patients? It is an old dilemma of psychotherapists that they must sit with their patients in the shaky boat and at the same time stand on the safe shore and wave at them encouragingly.

After years as a practicing logotherapist I have made a list of qualifications and attitudes that seem to me desirable. The result was surprising because it was a list of contradictions, yet a common thread runs through it all.

1. The Logotherapist Must Be Pessimistic and Optimistic. The logotherapeutic admonition, "Take people as they are and help them become what they could be," sounds optimistic; even more so if we attribute to human beings an extra dimension, the spiritual, which lifts them above other life forms and enables them to overcome misfortune. But of course logotherapists must not stick their heads in the sand; they must be pessimistic enough to recognize reality, to accept it as it is, and to explore the causes and facts that constitute the patient's problems.

Logotherapy attracts therapists who believe in human goodness. Cynics are not interested in logotherapy. But idealism, optimism, and belief in human nature are not enough to be a responsible logotherapist. Not every illness has psychosomatic causes, not every depression is noogenic, and not every psychically ill patient suffers from an existential vacuum.

Logotherapists, like other therapists, are obliged to gather all information that serves to interpret a situation. They have to be aware of possible misinterpretations and must not overestimate their abilities: referrals to other branches of the medical professions are sometimes necessary. Two case histories will illustrate this point.

Case # 32:

Mrs. B was an adult woman complaining of chest pains. Since the pain increased at times of psychological stress and no organic symptom could be found, the diagnosis "psychogenic" seemed reasonable. The pain diminished with relaxation exercises and logotherapeutic conversation. Finally it disappeared.

Six months later Mrs. B returned complaining about pain in the lower right stomach area. Her family doctor smilingly talked about nerves and sent her to me.

I am afraid of organically caused pain erroneously referred to the psychologist who, under such circumstances, is bound to fail. I was pessimistic enough to send Mrs. B first to another physician. Lo and behold, this physician who was unbiased and did not know that she ever had psychogenic disturbances, easily diagnosed gall stones. Without my pessimism precious time would have been lost.

Case # 33:

I substituted for a sick psychologist in charge of children in our counseling center. One patient was a girl whose teacher had complained that she was masturbating in class and had asked my colleague for help. The class psychologist thought the girl needed analytical play therapy, and that's what she got.

I had her examined by a medical doctor. It turned out that she had a chronic vaginal inflammation. For *that* reason she fidgeted in school and scratched between her legs. Yet for six months she had been treated with play therapy. Appropriate medication brought relief within two months.

Logotherapists must be pessimistic enough to suspect factual reasons behind the façade of symptoms. A frustrated search for meaning and a lack of motivation must not be assumed as the sole cause of sickness while there is the remotest possibility that other determinants may play a part.

Caution must also be exercised when a prognosis is made. Logotherapists must not simply don their rose-colored glasses and predict, even less promise, a quick recovery. Many setbacks are caused by the bitter disappointment of an unsuccessful therapy, and it is better to predict setbacks and minimize their importance than to exclude the possibility and to risk loss of credibility with the patient.

Logotherapists differ from most of their colleagues in their belief that a chance of recovery exists in spite of circumstances. The logotherapeutic creed is that every human being, through the resources of the spirit, has the chance—despite past, personal makeup and inherited genes—to change his or her life and fill it with meaning.

It's a wonderful thought, yet again and again I am overcome with doubts and inclined to give up a client as "hopeless." Yet every time I make a special effort not to deny the patient his chance. Sometimes, when desperate, I turn to other patients who are searching for meaning, and tell them my problem (without identifying the person concerned) and let them find arguments I can use. Many times my clients help me, giving me at the same time a lesson in optimism.

Case #34:

A 35-year-old woman, Mrs. R, came to me because of her existential frustration. Her husband had died eight years ago and left her with a small child. She lived in modest circumstances, a homemaker leading an unexciting life. She never went on vacation, rarely left her house, and had few friends and experiences.

She was dissatisfied with her life, critical, in perpetual bad humor, and hence unattractive to others, who avoided her.

In long sessions I tried to lead her to see some meaning potentials in her life: professional, social, leisure activities. Even a savings plan was discussed to make short vacations possible. But she found something wrong with every idea.

One day it was I who was disheartened. A young girl with whom I had worked for a long time, had become involved in crime. I felt in no frame of mind now, on top of it all, to put up with the usual negativism of the frustrated woman. So I told Mrs. R that this time we would not discuss her situation but that of another patient. I would appreciate her comments. I then told her of the girl and my fear that she would not recover from her criminal involvement.

But now my patient found words of comfort and optimism! "The present situation," she said, "may just be a passing phase. Some have to fall before they can rise. I would not condemn her like everyone else, but let her know that you are willing to assist her in the future if she wants it." I thanked Mrs. R and recognized that she, in saying what she did, had also helped herself—it was the first time in a long period of negativism that she had adopted a positive stance. From then on it became easier for us to look more positively at her own situation (which was much less difficult than that of the girl) and find clues for changes in a direction meaningful to her.

The logotherapist *listens* to her patients and learns from them— she gives and takes. Therapy cannot be carried out from books but must be developed from the words of the patient and, more important, from what lies behind the words.

The logotherapist must be a mixture of an optimist and pessimist in many ways. She must see the patients' plight but must believe they can move beyond. She sees severe limitations in some situations, but believes to the end that there exists at least one chance. She knows the patients' weaknesses, yet treats her clients as fully acceptable persons. She recognizes the fetters of childhood and education, yet helps patients to liberate themselves from these straitjackets. She knows about the patients' limitations of action, but encourages their responsibility to act within these limitations. Fanatics, who always need a scapegoat, will not like this attitude;

they prefer to blame society, politics, and all civilization for ruining a person's life. To blame is easier than to work things out.

I mistrust reformers who begin their reforms by accusing. It is our own weaknesses we see most clearly in others. Before we accuse, we'd better look at ourselves. Those who will not acknowledge their belief in a last island of unconditional freedom in the human spirit, must forego logotherapy. But then they also must be willing to accept themselves as products of mere chance.

II. The Logotherapist Must Explore Causes and Ignore Causes. The logotherapist must ignore causes, especially those that cannot be changed and if dwelling on them produces more harm than good. If you keep reminding a child that grew up in an orphanage that he was abandoned and that, because of his early childhood experiences, he will never amount to anything, you make him a mental cripple—which is not foreordained. It is unpardonable even to indicate to a handicapped woman that her handicap is the cause of her failures, although there may well be a connection. Nor should the young or the elderly be permitted to use age as an excuse for foolish actions. Some connections are better left alone; if too much attention is paid to them, they can paralyze the human spirit that can defy those connections.

Case # 35:

A married couple was in despair because their 4-year-old foster son liked to play games wearing women's clothing. The child had come from the slums and they feared he had a genetic disposition toward homosexuality. They watched his every move and interpreted every word in that light. They were shocked by such harmless comments as, "Daddy is much gooder than mummy." Had the boy been their own, they probably would have paid little attention to his games and comments. But their worry about his possibly harmful genetic background was felt by the child. He noticed the special attention given him when he put on mother's skirt; he felt important, and repeated the act.

The child's background may well have been the reason for his conduct, yet my advice to the parents was to ignore it. In my talks to them I did not dwell on the alleged abnormal tendencies of the child. I did not claim that the child's behavior was normal but proposed to the parents to treat him as if he were. "Don't pay much attention when he puts on a skirt and expresses preferences for his father's affection," I told them. "Build up the father as a model. Let father work with the boy around the house, let the boy watch when father washes the car, tell him stories about brave men. Tell him that he might become such a man himself one day." I asked them to treat the boy as if he were their own natural child.

The foster parents did this, and after some time the symptoms disappeared. I cannot tell what caused the odd interest in women's clothing but the "abnormal genes" could have done a lot of damage if they had continued to preoccupy the parents.

Causes sometimes must be ignored even if they obtrude themselves on the therapist. Go easy when you have a premature "aha!" experience during the first sessions, and look with caution at "obvious causes" presented by the client.

A mother told me, "Our little daughter is afraid of the dark. Unfortunately she was present when Grandma was found dead in bed, and ever since she is afraid of the dark." The explanation seemed plausible. But on further inquiry it turned out that the little girl had been afraid of the dark even before her grandmother died, and had wanted to sleep only when the light was on. I discovered that the child had been not all that fond of her grandmother and felt it was actually "quite good" that she had gone to heaven. Therapists, generally, are willing to spend a lot of time to search for causes, but sometimes they have to summon the courage to ignore them. It is not the logotherapist's task to uncover causes at any price but only where it serves a purpose. And sometimes a better purpose is served by ignoring causes.

A related contradiction in logotherapeutic practice concerns the patients: They must learn to accept their fate, and they must also learn to fight their fate. In short: Be able to accept; be determined to resist.

How the logotherapist deals with the patients' causes of illness will influence their approaches in overcoming the illness. When causes cannot be changed, the logotherapist will ignore them and the patient must learn to live with them. When causes *can* be changed, the logotherapist will attempt to explore them and to activate the patient's forces to combat them. In the first case, the logotherapist might try modification of attitudes or dereflection; in the second, paradoxical intention or strengthening of the will.

A wise saying goes, "Half of our misfortune is avoidable, the other half is based on a wrong interpretation of life." It is not always possible to avoid misfortune or interpret misfortune in an acceptable way. Nevertheless these are the directions logotherapists will keep in mind.

"Be able to accept, be determined to resist," is a precept not popular today. People in our civilization are spoiled. They cannot accept suffering, they rebel against their fate, they insist on their "right" to live a pleasurable life, and become aggressive-hysterical when faced with hardship. How can such people face illness and death? How can they stand up to economic setbacks, unemployment, and want? Some conditions can and need to be fought. But it is a great gift to be able to accept the unavoidable, to have the courage to defy one's weaknesses, to overcome one's insecurities, to rise above one's greed, to transcend oneself. One need not yield to every temptation, fall into depression because of a disappointment, scream at every provocation, and practice oneupmanship at every opportunity.

To ignore causes and yet tolerate them, to explore causes and fight them—this is a great contradiction in the concept of logotherapy.

III. The logotherapist must be able to understand patients who never had a chance for a healthy development, and also those who had all their chances and did not use them. What is easier: to feel for a youngster who grew up in a slum sharing a crowded apartment with many siblings, who never knew his father, got poor schooling, never had a job, and finally became a petty thief; or for a middle-class youngster who received loving care from his family, good schooling, had many job opportunities, yet got into trouble for senseless thievery? The first arouses sympathy, the second is hard to understand and easy to condemn.

In our counseling center we see both kinds: the unemployed, the welfare recipients, alcoholics, gypsies, exhibitionists, prostitutes, and well-off neurotics, executives whose children flunk out of school, aging artists who suffer from depression, doctors' suicidal wives, students who suffer from existential frustration.

Work with the underprivileged is difficult but holds an element of satisfaction. The therapist knows about the patients' unhappy living conditions, tries to counteract them as far as possible, and is proud when small improvements occur. In such cases the therapist knows the foe and fully understands why the patient failed. It is like repairing a broken vase: the pieces are carefully picked up and glued together in the hope that it will last. Such repair work includes help in job hunting, finding a place to live, getting child-care, legal advice, and plain advice on living. Here the therapists expect a minimum from the patients and a maximum from themselves.

Work with the middle- and upper-class is different. The patients live in affluence, have no worries about job opportunities or housing, are able to satisfy most of their wishes, and are usually surrounded by people who care. They develop their neuroses and depressions without apparent cause, are not interested in minor improvements, do not themselves know what they want, but nothing is good enough. The therapists do not know the foe—the beautiful vase is smashed, but there is no point piecing it together because repaired stuff is too inferior for this kind of clientele.

Therapists must try to understand these patients too—the unfounded upsets, the senseless suffering, the macabre egoism. Sometimes I suspect that I cease to be a good logotherapist because I simply cannot muster enough understanding.

To Case #29:

"You stand among the flowers and water the weeds," I once told the patient, and she laughed. "That's exactly what I do," she said.

"Why?" I kept asking. "Why?"

"That's why I come to you," she said. "You water the flowers, I water the weeds."

The woman had everything she could wish for—a loving husband, healthy children, a high standard of living, a beautiful home, and many possibilities to do meaningful work. Many of my lower-class patients wouldn't have dared dream about all this. Yet the woman lay in bed for hours and let herself be pitied by concerned friends and relatives. One might have suspected she did not want to be cured, that she needed her condition to remain the center of attention. Whoever visited this family did not inquire about the children or the husband's work—only about the health of Mrs. X.

A show was made of tending the weeds and of trampling the flowers so others could bring more flowers.

Logotherapists are equipped to help those who have all the advantages because their understanding of human nature makes them sensitive to the destructive force of meaninglessness behind the symptoms.

Meaning can come from activities. People who work regular hours tend to be more stable than idle ones. Work is an important factor of our physical health. Statistics show the health hazard for the idle young, those who are "only" housewives, the retired, the handicapped, the wealthy. *Having* money does not contribute to physical health. *Earning* money does.

Idle people are found among the extreme poor and the extreme rich. Some cannot find work, others don't need to find it. Those who cannot find work suffer from a lack of growth for which they are only partly responsible. But those who are idle because they need not work lack social understanding and show an egotism for which they alone are responsible.

Logotherapists may see their efforts fail in fighting this senseless and destructive egotism, but they must give their support and sympathy to these unhappy people.

IV. Logotherapists must have their own value system, yet fully accept the value system of their patients. It is generally understood that psychotherapists accept the patient's value system unless it is unhealthy. They respect the patient's religious, political, and moral views without passing judgment, even when they differ from their own. Atheistic therapists, for instance, will discuss matters of faith with members of orthodox denominations. Therapists must be flexible enough to answer questions in such a way that they neither deny their own beliefs nor shake the belief of their patients. The Socratic dialogue is the proper vehicle to answer questions with questions, and thus help patients find their own answers.

Logotherapists, however, have an additional obligation. They also *give* answers, and these derive from their own value system which must range over a wide spectrum. They need an ample reservoir from which to draw even in the most delicate cases. For example, questions about God can hardly be avoided in many therapeutic exchanges. It would make no sense to say that logotherapists should belong to a specific religion, yet they must have some concept of the divine. It may merely be the belief in the goodness of humankind, in the true and the beautiful. These represent a communication bridge to the believer. In politics, too, the therapist may have specific alignments and yet understand the positive goals of opposition parties. There always is a meeting ground if one's own value system is broad enough to dispense with dogma.

I have been able to help patients who believed in the literal existence of the devil, and others who denied the existence of a higher power in any form. I am reminded of a case, quoted by Frankl, of an Orthodox Jew who was in despair because he had lost his sons in concentration camps and was unable to have any more children. During the course of the therapy sessions it became clear that his misery centered around his belief that he was prevented from being reunited with his children in heaven. According to his faith, his children, having died innocently, would go to heaven which would be barred to him, an earthly sinner. By applying his patient's beliefs, which Frankl himself did not share, he was able to bring about a change of attitudes in the old man. By quoting passages from the Talmud, Frankl helped him see a possible meaning behind his suffering: It is written in the Good Book that our tears are saved for the Day of Judgment. Was it not conceivable that God had demanded the old man's great sufferings so he would be admitted to heaven and thus see his children again?

While logotherapists must be able to accept their patients' meaning concepts, they must say "no" to value systems that reflect reductionism, pandeterminism, and nihilism. "No, it is not true that you are nothing but an animal that has to respond to its instincts."—"No, it is not true that you are a helpless victim of your past."—"No, it is not true that nothing matters because nothing is real." Logotherapists must use their own value systems to help patients see that, although they *are* instinctual, victims of circumstances, and that negative forces operate in them and the world, they *can* take a stand against all these drawbacks.

Beyond such exceptions, logotherapists must be able to draw

from their own values without inflicting them on the patient, and be tolerant enough to put their own views into the terminology and concepts of the patient. It is vital that the patient understands, and if understanding is helped by using the word "devil" for "illness," or "evil" for "disaster," then the logotherapist is well advised to use these words.

High on the list of the logotherapist's values is his concern for the patients. But we must not overestimate our capacities. Many ills cure themselves, and many suggestions offered in good faith cannot be used by the patient. We must learn from failures but not take credit for every success. We must be aware of the self-healing powers of our patients and their ability to mobilize these powers to improve their lives. By the same token, people are free to decide against therapeutic help, against their recovery, against their "only chance." This, too, we must respect, even when it hurts. We cannot do more than place our efforts for the patient high on our scale of values—the final responsibility remains with the patient.

The value system of the logotherapist plays an important part in another area. What we tell our patients is evidence of our own life philosophy. We must be willing to act according to our advice to our patients. We reveal ourselves as genuine to the degree that we stand behind our words.

If we are to help our patients, our genuineness must be apparent. But it contains a contradiction: We must acknowledge our continuing search for meaning, and also show that we have found fulfillment. This contradiction, too, can be resolved because nobody's search for meaning is ever concluded and fulfillment reached once and for all. We keep searching all our lives, and logotherapists must not be ashamed to admit it.

This book would not have been written except for a minor event that clarified for me the task of sharing my experiences. I had procrastinated, with lack of time and family responsibilities as excuses. Actually I was scared of the idea of writing a book and also hesitated to plunge into the work connected with it.

Then, one day, I noticed my first gray hair. This is no tragedy but I was touched by the breath of transitoriness. I still feel young, have many plans for the future, but time passes. I remembered the advice I had given to a client two years ago.

Case # 36:

Mrs. H was 29 and had started to dye her hair since she discovered her first gray hair at the age of 25. She had developed a strong allergy against the dye and was in danger of losing her hair if she continued to dye it. She became so desperate that she considered suicide. I attempted a modification of attitudes and drew her attention to the fact that the first gray hair can be seen as a warning sign: time is passing. Stop postponing. Do what you want to do now. Usually, the warning comes later, but at 25 it gave her more time to do things.

She began to see her gray hair with new eyes: not a reminder of aging but of things she still wanted to do. She started rug weaving, a hobby she had postponed, traveled, took courses. Since she considered aging as an impulse to live, she never thought of death any more.

I thought of Mrs. H. "This is the test of my own logotherapy," I thought. "Do I accept my own advice? Do I stand behind it?"

I wrote my book. My first gray hair had told me: "If you want to write a book, start now. Tomorrow might be too late."

This is perhaps the best advice the "ideal" logotherapist can give to patients: "It is never too late to begin to fill your life with meaning and become healthy in the process."

Selected Grove Press Paperbacks

62480-7   ACKER, KATHY / Great Expectations: A Novel / $6.95
17458-5   ALLEN, DONALD & BUTTERICK, GEORGE F., eds. / The Postmoderns: The New American Poetry Revised / $9.95
17397-X   ANONYMOUS / My Secret Life / $4.95
62433-5   BARASH, D. and LIPTON, J. / Stop Nuclear War! A Handbook / $7.95
17087-3   BARNES, JOHN / Evita—First Lady: A Biography of Eva Peron / $4.95
17208-6   BECKETT, SAMUEL / Endgame / $3.50
17299-X   BECKETT, SAMUEL / Three Novels: Molloy, Malone Dies and The Unnamable / $6.95
17204-3   BECKETT, SAMUEL / Waiting for Godot / $3.95
62064-X   BECKETT, SAMUEL / Worstward Ho / $5.95
17244-2   BORGES, JORGE LUIS / Ficciones / $6.95
17112-8   BRECHT, BERTOLT / Galileo / $3.95
17106-3   BRECHT, BERTOLT / Mother Courage and Her Children / $2.95
17393-7   BRETON ANDRE / Nadja / $6.95
17439-9   BULGAKOV, MIKHAIL / The Master and Margarita / $5.95
17108-X   BURROUGHS, WILLIAM S. / Naked Lunch / $4.95
17749-5   BURROUGHS, WILLIAM S. / The Soft Machine, Nova Express, The Wild Boys: Three Novels / $5.95
62488-2   CLARK, AL, ed. / The Film Year Book 1984 / $12.95
17535-2   COWARD, NOEL / Three Plays (Private Lives, Hay Fever, Blithe Spirit) / $7.95
17219-1   CUMMINGS, E.E. / 100 Selected Poems / $3.95
17327-9   FANON, FRANZ / The Wretched of the Earth / $4.95
17483-6   FROMM, ERICH / The Forgotten Language / $6.95
17390-2   GENET, JEAN / The Maids and Deathwatch: Two Plays / $8.95
17838-6   GENET, JEAN / Querelle / $4.95
17662-6   GERVASI, TOM / Arsenal of Democracy II / $12.95
17956-0   GETTLEMAN, MARVIN, et.al. eds. / El Salvador: Central America in the New Cold War / $9.95
17648-0   GIRODIAS, MAURICE, ed. / The Olympia Reader / $5.95
62490-4   GUITAR PLAYER MAGAZINE / The Guitar Player Book (Revised and Updated Edition) $11.95
62003-8   HITLER, ADOLF / Hitler's Secret Book / $7.95
17125-X   HOCHHUTH, ROLF / The Deputy / $7.95
62115-8   HOLMES, BURTON / The Olympian Games in Athens, 1896 / $6.95

17209-4 IONESCO, EUGENE / Four Plays (The Bald Soprano, The Lesson, The Chairs, and Jack or The Submission) / $6.95
17226-4 IONESCO, EUGENE / Rhinoceros / $5.95
62123-9 JOHNSON, CHARLES / Oxherding Tale / $6.95
17254-X KEENE, DONALD, ed. / Modern Japanese Literature / $12.50
17952-8 KEROUAC, JACK / The Subterraneans / $3.50
62424-6 LAWRENCE, D.H. / Lady Chatterley's Lover / $3.95
17016-4 MAMET, DAVID / American Buffalo / $4.95
17760-6 MILLER, HENRY / Tropic of Cancer / $4.95
17295-7 MILLER, HENRY / Tropic of Capricorn / $3.95
17869-6 NERUDA, PABLO / Five Decades: Poems 1925-1970. Bilingual ed. / $12.50
17092-X ODETS, CLIFFORD / Six Plays (Waiting for Lefty, Awake and Sing, Golden Boy, Rocket to the Moon, Till the Day I Die, Paradise Lost) / $7.95
17650-2 OE, KENZABURO / A Personal Matter / $6.95
17232-9 PINTER, HAROLD / The Birthday Party & The Room / $6.95
17251-5 PINTER, HAROLD / The Homecoming / $5.95
17539-5 POMERANCE, BERNARD / The Elephant Man / $5.95
17827-0 RAHULA, WALPOLA / What the Buddha Taught / $6.95
17658-8 REAGE, PAULINE / The Story of O, Part II; Return to the Chateau / $3.95
62169-7 RECHY, JOHN / City of Night / $4.50
62001-1 ROSSET, BARNEY and JORDAN, FRED, eds. / Evergreen Review No. 98 / $5.95
62498-X ROSSET, PETER and VANDERMEER, JOHN / The Nicaragua Reader / $9.95
17119-5 SADE, MARQUIS DE / The 120 Days of Sodom and Other Writings / $12.50
62009-7 SEGALL, J. PETER / Deduct This Book: How Not to Pay Taxes While Ronald Reagan is President / $6.95
17467-4 SELBY, HUBERT / Last Exit to Brooklyn / $3.95
17948-X SHAWN, WALLACE, and GREGORY, ANDRE / My Dinner with Andre / $6.95
17797-5 SNOW, EDGAR / Red Star Over China / $9.95
17260-4 STOPPARD, TOM / Rosencrantz and Guildenstern Are Dead / $3.95
17474-7 SUZUKI, D.T. / Introduction to Zen Buddhism / $3.95
17599-9 THELWELL, MICHAEL / The Harder They Come: A Novel about Jamaica / $7.95
17969-2 TOOLE, JOHN KENNEDY / A Confederacy of Dunces / $4.50
17418-6 WATTS, ALAN W. / The Spirit of Zen / $3.95

GROVE PRESS, INC., 196 West Houston St., New York, N.Y. 10014